THE 1987 DEFENSE BUDGET

THE 1987 DEFENSE BUDGET

Joshua M. Epstein

THE BROOKINGS INSTITUTION

Washington, D.C.

THE BROOKINGS INSTITUTION is an independent organization devoted to nonpartisan research, education, and publication in economics, government, foreign policy, and the social sciences generally. Its principal purposes are to aid in the development of sound public policies and to promote public understanding of issues of national importance.

The Institution was founded on December 8, 1927, to merge the activities of the Institute for Government Research, founded in 1916, the Institute of Economics, founded in 1922, and the Robert Brookings Graduate School of Economics and Government, founded in 1924.

The Board of Trustees is responsible for the general administration of the Institution, while the immediate direction of the policies, program, and staff is vested in the President, assisted by an advisory committee of the officers and staff. The by-laws of the Institution state: "It is the function of the Trustees to make possible the conduct of scientific research, and publication, under the most favorable conditions, and to safeguard the independence of the research staff in the pursuit of their studies and in the publication of the results of such studies. It is not a part of their function to determine, control, or influence the conduct of particular investigations or the conclusions reached."

The President bears final responsibility for the decision to publish a manuscript as a Brookings book. In reaching his judgment on the competence, accuracy, and objectivity of each study, the President is advised by the director of the appropriate research program and weighs the views of a panel of expert outside readers who report to him in confidence on the quality of the work. Publication of a work signifies that it is deemed a competent treatment worthy of public consideration but does not imply endorsement of conclusions or recommendations.

The Institution maintains its position of neutrality on issues of public policy in order to safeguard the intellectual freedom of the staff. Hence interpretations or conclusions in Brookings publications should be understood to be solely those of the authors and should not be attributed to the Institution, to its trustees, officers, or other staff members, or to the organizations that support its research.

FOREWORD

THE CURRENT intense pressure to reduce the federal deficit creates grave risks that defense spending will be cut indiscriminately. There is widespread concern that the Gramm-Rudman-Hollings automatic formula for restraining defense expenditures would be at best inefficient, and at worst might actually damage national security. At the same time, most lawmakers find unacceptable the Reagan administration's proposals to continue a military buildup while reducing the deficit without raising taxes. Against this background, there is a pressing need for reasonable alternatives both to the administration's defense plan and to the military budget that would be produced through the Gramm-Rudman-Hollings procedure.

In this study, Joshua M. Epstein, a research associate in the Brookings Foreign Policy Studies program, identifies several problems in the administration's defense proposals and presents an alternative multiyear defense plan. After rigorously assessing U.S. nuclear and conventional requirements, he offers specific recommendations that over four years would cost $117 billion less than the administration's plan without endangering U.S. or allied security.

The author acknowledges the valuable suggestions of John D. Steinbruner, William B. Quandt, Barry R. Posen, Paul B. Stares, Martin Binkin, Charles L. Schultze, Lawrence J. Korb, and Russell Murray 2nd. He also extends thanks to Jeanette Morrison for editing the manuscript, to Lisa B. Mages for research assistance, to James E. McKee for verifying references and tables, and to Ann M. Ziegler for secretarial assistance.

This study was funded by grants from the Ford Foundation and the John D. and Catherine T. MacArthur Foundation.

The views expressed here are those of the author and should not be ascribed to the persons or foundations whose assistance is acknowledged above or to the trustees, officers, or other staff members of the Brookings Institution.

BRUCE K. MACLAURY
President

May 1986
Washington, D.C.

THE 1987 DEFENSE BUDGET

A PRIME responsibility of government is "to provide for the common defense." But since resources are finite, it is critical that national security requirements be met as efficiently as possible. Any rational attempt to satisfy them efficiently must be based on a determination of military needs. One way to approach the perennial question, "How much is enough?" is to specify the basic missions for which one's forces are structured, to assess their likely performance in executing those missions, and to identify the most economical solutions to whatever problems are thereby identified, eliminating unnecessary expenditures where possible.

Following a review of the Reagan administration's budget request, and of certain structural budget constraints peculiar to defense, an analysis along those lines, of strategic and conventional requirements, is undertaken below. It demonstrates that substantial defense spending reductions can be made without detriment to national security. Or, to put it differently, deficit reduction need not entail security reduction. However, deficit reduction *will* entail security reduction if effected under the Balanced Budget and Emergency Deficit Control Act of 1985.

Gramm-Rudman-Hollings

Sponsored by Republicans Phil Gramm and Warren B. Rudman and Democrat Ernest F. Hollings, the act established an automatic procedure to eliminate the federal deficit by the end of fiscal 1991. The deficit targets under Gramm-Rudman-Hollings are shown in table 1.

If in any year the deficit exceeds the target (by more than $10 billion in fiscal 1987 through 1990), automatic reductions, or sequestrations,

1

Table 1. Gramm-Rudman-Hollings Federal Deficit Targets, Fiscal Years 1986–91
Billions of dollars

Year	Target	Year	Target
1986	171.9	1989	72.0
1987	144.0	1990	36.0
1988	108.0	1991	0

Source: Pub. L. No. 99-177, sec. 201(a), 99 Stat. 1037, 1039.

are triggered to eliminate the entire excess. These cuts in federal outlays are to be split 50–50 between defense and nondefense spending. Within defense, equal percentage cuts in outlays are applied to each program, without reference to America's global commitments, without any analysis of military requirements, and with virtually no flexibility to allocate reductions in accordance with national priorities, or even to cut "lemons" more than proven weapons.[1] In short, defense spending reductions under Gramm-Rudman-Hollings are totally divorced from that effort to calibrate means and ends that is associated with the term "rationality." In addition, if Congress does nothing to avoid them and the deficit is big enough, these automatic cuts could be huge, up to $30 billion in actual

1. Automatic reduction under Gramm-Rudman-Hollings involves three steps. Step 1: Compute total outlays resulting from budgetary resources (new budget authority plus unobligated prior-year balances). In lieu of yet-to-be developed "combined outlay rates" for budgetary resources, the outlay rates for budget authority may be used. Step 2: Form the ratio of the total defense sequester (one-half the amount by which projected deficits exceed the Gramm-Rudman-Hollings deficit target) to the outlay total computed in step 1. This yields the uniform percentage by which each program, project, and activity is to be reduced in outlays. Step 3: Reduce budgetary resources by the same percentage rate. But within budgetary resources, there is freedom to distribute the cut between new budget authority and prior-year unobligated balances. Under the Gramm-Rudman-Hollings trigger, therefore, the reduction in budget authority proper is indeterminate up to this variable percentage of unobligated prior-year balances. For further details, see *Increasing the Statutory Limit on the Public Debt*, H. Rept. 99-433, 99 Cong. 1 sess. (Government Printing Office, 1985); and Alice C. Maroni and Robert E. Foelber, *The Gramm-Rudman-Hollings Deficit Reduction Process (P.L. 99-177) and the Department of Defense: A Summary Review*, Congressional Research Service, Library of Congress, Report 86-7 F (January 6, 1986). For a complete breakdown of Gramm-Rudman-Hollings's effect on the fiscal 1986 budget, see Office of Management and Budget (OMB) and Congressional Budget Office (CBO), "Sequestration Report for Fiscal Year 1986—A Joint Report to the Comptroller General of the United States," *Federal Register*, vol. 51, bk. 2 (January 15, 1986), pp. 1917–2336; or Alice C. Maroni and Robert E. Foelber, "The Gramm-Rudman-Hollings Sequestration Process for FY 1986: A Summary of DOD Elements in the OMB/CBO and GAO Sequestration Reports," Congressional Research Service, Library of Congress, Report 86-16 F (January 27, 1986).

Table 2. **Reagan Administration Five-Year Defense Budget, Fiscal Years 1987–91**[a]

Billions of dollars

Item	1987	1988	1989	1990	1991
Budget authority[b]	311.6	332.4	353.5	374.7	395.5
Outlays					
As submitted by administration[b]	274.3	290.7	313.3	335.5	356.6
As computed by author[c]	288.5	307.8	325.8	345.1	365.1
Discrepancy[d]	14.3	17.1	12.5	9.6	8.5

a. Figures are for Defense Department military functions (051 account) and exclude defense-related activities of the Department of Energy. Figures are rounded.

b. *Historical Tables, Budget of the United States Government, Fiscal Year 1987*, tables 3.3, 5.1.

c. The author's outlays are calculated from the president's budget authority, using the outlay rates published by the Defense Department in *Financial Summary Tables, Department of Defense Budget for Fiscal Year 1987* (DOD, 1986), tab M.

d. Fiscal 1987 has been rounded up from $14.265 billion. These represent minimum discrepancies, since the *Financial Summary Tables* give only net, not gross, outlay rates. If the latter are used the discrepancy grows to $14.8 billion in fiscal 1987 and totals $66 billion over the five years.

defense spending (outlays) in fiscal 1987, an 18 percent cut across the board demanding military personnel reductions of 300,000 to half a million.[2]

The budget submitted to Congress by the Reagan administration purports to avoid triggering these automatic reductions, allegedly reducing the federal deficit to $144 billion in fiscal 1987, the Gramm-Rudman-Hollings target for that year.

Underlying the administration's claim to having met the Gramm-Rudman-Hollings target is its estimate of Defense Department outlays for fiscal 1987; that estimate is $274.3 billion dollars (see table 2). In fact, this number is not consistent with the administration's own budget authority request to Congress and the Defense Department's published outlay rates. Those, official, data yield defense outlays $14 billion to $15 billion higher than the administration's number for fiscal 1987, levels which (other things fixed) would trigger Gramm-Rudman-Hollings. Over the five-year period, the administration appears to have underestimated true outlays by more than $60 billion (see table 2).

Under the administration's plan, Defense appropriations for fiscal

2. Jonathan Fuerbringer, "Senator Sees a 1987 Budget without Tax Increase," *New York Times*, January 23, 1986; based on the Congressional Budget Office's estimate (since revised down to $181 billion) of a $200 billion deficit for 1987. The $181 billion figure is from CBO, *The Economic and Budget Outlook: Fiscal Years 1987–1991* (CBO, 1986), p. xiv. For a recent estimate of the impact on defense of automatic reductions under Gramm-Rudman-Hollings, see Tom Donnelly, "Evangelical Aspin Preaches to the Unbelievers; Other Lawmakers Impassive about Gramm-Rudman," *Defense News*, March 24, 1986.

1987 would grow by 8.5 percent in real terms over their fiscal 1986 levels. Since no tax increase is proposed, the growth in defense would be financed primarily through sharp cuts in many nondefense domestic programs, some of which would have to be eliminated outright. In the past, budgets mandating social spending cuts of this magnitude have been "dead on arrival" in Congress; in this election year, pressures to reject such cuts are especially powerful.

If Congress restores monies in these nondefense areas without compensatory reductions in defense, or increased taxes, the deficit will exceed—or *further* exceed—the $144 billion target, triggering militarily mindless cuts under Gramm-Rudman-Hollings. If tax increases are ruled out as the president insists, then Congress's choices are indeed unattractive. Is there an alternative? Perhaps, if the United States can meet its fundamental security requirements without 8.5 percent real growth for fiscal 1987, a possibility this study examines in detail.

Finally, even if the Supreme Court finds key provisions of Gramm-Rudman-Hollings—specifically, the role of the comptroller general—to be unconstitutional, lawmakers will be under extreme pressure to reduce the federal deficit. Regardless of the Court's decision, moreover, the Gramm-Rudman-Hollings deficit *targets* will powerfully shape Congress's attempt to control defense spending.

Anatomy of the Defense Budget

To appreciate some of the structural constraints under which that attempt will operate, with or without Gramm-Rudman-Hollings, some basic mechanics of defense spending need to be understood.

Relationships between Budget Authority and Outlays

There are several classes of "money" in defense; the two most fundamental are budget authority and outlays. (A third, obligations, is discussed below under the topic of rescissions.) Budget authority is akin to a checking account and represents the amount the Pentagon is allowed to spend. It is, precisely, the value of spending obligations, or contracts, into which the Pentagon is legally authorized to enter. It is new budget authority that Congress appropriates each year. Outlays are the actual expenditures made by the Pentagon in a given year. Different categories

Table 3. Defense Outlay Rates by Appropriation Title

Percent of first-year budget authority

	Year					
Appropriation title	*First*	*Second*	*Third*	*Fourth*	*Fifth*	*Sixth*[a]
Military personnel	97.79	1.49	0.05	0	0	0
Operation and maintenance	73.02	21.03	2.69	0	0	0
Procurement	14.64	31.32	26.69	13.35	6.73	0.42
Research, development, test, and evaluation	46.62	40.33	7.96	1.74	0	0
Military construction	12.91	36.09	25.96	10.35	7.71	2.61
Family housing	46.36	29.56	13.49	3.57	1.80	0.82

Source: Department of Defense, *Financial Summary Tables, Fiscal Year 1987*, tab M. Not shown are outlay rates for special foreign currency program and Defense-wide contingencies.

a. Sixth-year spendout rates are not given for the current fiscal year in the *Financial Summary Tables*, though they are given for the preceding year. For fiscal 1987 procurement, military construction, and family housing, the sixth-year outlay rates are estimated assuming the same sixth-year total lapsed-funding percentage (cents on the dollar not spent) as exhibited by the six-year outlay rates beginning in fiscal 1986, which are given in the *Financial Summary Tables* for fiscal 1987.

of the defense budget have different outlay rates. These are shown in table 3.

Of a dollar of budget authority appropriated for procurement, only about 15 cents will actually be spent in the first year, 31 cents in the second, and 27 cents in the third; procurement is relatively "slow" money. By contrast, a dollar of budget authority for operation and maintenance will be all but spent after two years, with 73 cents laid out in the very first year; operation and maintenance is relatively "fast" money.

Deficits, of course, are a function of outlays, not budget authority. Congress, however, appropriates the latter, not the former. With table 3 as background, it is easy to see why the fast-money accounts (associated most closely with the readiness of forces) should be the most vulnerable when deficit reduction becomes a congressional imperative. A dollar cut from procurement budget authority reduces outlays (and the deficit, other things being equal) a mere 15 cents in the first fiscal year, while a dollar cut in operation-and-maintenance budget authority saves fully 73 cents in outlays.

By the same logic, however, these outlay rates mean that slow-money investment accounts, such as procurement, must be reduced *today* if they are to contribute to the reduction of outlays in future years. Otherwise, multiyear deficit reduction (for example, intended to avoid triggering Gramm-Rudman-Hollings in the future) will require that the

Table 4. Outlays If Budget Authority Were Zero for Fiscal Years 1987–91
Millions of dollars

Appropriation title	1987	1988	1989	1990	1991
Military personnel	1,042	34	0	0	0
Operation and maintenance	17,834	2,013	0	0	0
Procurement	72,034	43,782	19,243	6,639	389
Research and development	16,567	3,230	587	0	0
Military construction	4,281	2,407	1,090	551	138
Family housing	1,380	551	174	74	23
Other	519	165	44	7	0
Total	113,657	52,184	21,137	7,272	550

Sources: Computed using budget authority data for fiscal 1982–86 from *Historical Tables, Budget of the United States Government, Fiscal Year 1987*, table 5.1, and outlay rates from Department of Defense, *Financial Summary Tables, Fiscal Year 1987*, tab M. Each entry is obtained by applying to each appropriation title its outlay rates beginning in 1982 (the earliest year with an outlay impact on 1987) and letting the budget authority spend out, holding budget authority at zero from fiscal 1987 forward. Figures are rounded.

fast-money operating and support accounts be repeatedly plundered, the end result being an inevitable decline in readiness. This effect will be exacerbated by the existence of large spending backlogs that are controllable only through extraordinary measures.

The Backlog

Because appropriations made in one year may require many years to "spend out," there is always a backlog of actual spending to which the Pentagon is committed from budget authority granted in prior years. Indeed, considerable spending would occur even if total budget authority were held literally to zero (see table 4). Even if new budget authority were literally zero for each year (that is, if Congress appropriated zero budget authority), five-year outlays would nevertheless total $194.8 billion, a nontrivial sum.

For any appropriation title, the actual outlays in 1987 will be the sum of outlays from prior-year budget authority, plus the first-year outlay for fiscal 1987 budget authority; amounts in fiscal 1988 will include the second year of fiscal 1987 money and the first year of fiscal 1988, and so forth. This cumulation is illustrated for the procurement account in table 5.

In turn, the prior-year backlog for any fiscal year is the year's total outlays, net of outlays generated by current budget authority. Over the defense budget as a whole, the prior-year backlogs for fiscal 1987–91 are estimated in table 6.

Table 5. Outlay Budget for Procurement, Fiscal Years 1987–91
Millions of dollars

Item	1987	1988	1989	1990	1991
Budget authority	95,777	102,400	112,030	118,805	125,946
Outlays from budget authority granted:					
Prior to 1987	72,034	43,782	19,243	6,639	389
In 1987	14,022	29,997	25,563	12,786	6,446
In 1988	. . .	14,991	32,072	27,331	13,670
In 1989	. . .	. . .	16,401	35,088	29,901
In 1990	. . .	. . .	. . .	17,393	37,210
In 1991	. . .	. . .	. . .	. . .	18,438
Total yearly outlays	86,056	88,771[a]	93,279	99,237	106,054

Sources: Computed using budget authority data from *Historical Tables, Budget of the United States Government, Fiscal Year 1987*, table 5.1, and outlay rates from Department of Defense, *Financial Summary Tables, Fiscal Year 1987*, tab M. Total outlays, computed by applying the administration's outlay rates to its budget authority data, exceed the administration's submitted outlay estimates for procurement by the following amounts (in millions of dollars): $9,348 (fiscal 1987), $7,528 (fiscal 1988), $4,398 (fiscal 1989), $3,605 (fiscal 1990), and $2,115 (fiscal 1991), for a total of $26,994 over five years. For the administration's outlay estimates, see *Historical Tables, Budget of the United States Government, Fiscal Year 1987*, table 3.3.

a. Items do not total because of rounding.

The backlog represents almost 40 percent of current outlays. This is the amount that cannot be cut without rescission (discussed below). This built-in spending explains why *outlays will grow even if budget authority does not*. Indeed, to truly freeze actual spending, over a quarter of a trillion dollars would have to be cut from the Pentagon's five-year plan. This and other relationships are shown in table 7. In this light, claims that a freeze on budget authority will gut the defense buildup seem overdrawn. The same "momentum" carries with it a risk, however.

This backlog represents a serious constraint on the controllability of defense spending. Consider that, of a given year's outlays, nearly 40 percent is backlog spending, while roughly an additional 29 percent is allocated to military personnel, family housing, and management accounts. That leaves only about a third of the defense budget open to manipulation without cutting pay, people, or retirement. If the latter categories of spending are considered essentially off-limits, if rescission is ruled out, and if large deficit reductions (that is, outlay cuts) are to be made in the current year, the effect on the core readiness accounts will be devastating. The risk of a "hollow" force becomes very real, particularly given the Reagan administration's priorities. Thus far, investment (procurement, research and development, and military construction) has taken priority over operation and support (operation and

Table 6. The Overall Defense Budget Backlog, Fiscal Years 1987–91

Billions of dollars unless otherwise specified

Item	1987	1988	1989	1990	1991
Total outlays for year[a]	288.5	307.8	325.8	345.1	365.1
Outlays from current-year budget authority[b]	174.5	186.1	198.0	209.8	221.5
Outlays from prior-year budget authority[c]	114.0	121.7	127.8	135.3	143.6
Outlays from prior-year budget authority as a percentage of year's total outlays[d]	39.5	39.5	39.2	39.2	39.3

a. These are defense budget outlays (051 account) as computed by the author (see table 2).

b. Computed by multiplying each year's budget authority (see table 2) by the first-year aggregate spendout rate (the sum of the first year's spending for each appropriation title, divided by total budget authority). This rate equals 0.56 for fiscal 1987 and, for simplicity's sake, is assumed to maintain that value through fiscal 1991. See the appendix for a fuller discussion of aggregate outlay rates and their use.

c. Total outlays for year minus outlays from current-year budget authority.

d. If the same calculations are done from the administration's outlay numbers (see table 2), the backlog as a percentage appears to be lower: 36.4, 36.0, 36.8, 37.5, and 37.8 for fiscal 1987–91. Underestimating outlays has the effect of overestimating the controllability of defense spending.

maintenance, military personnel, and family housing). In fact, the ratio of operation and support expenditures to investment expenditures has been lower than at any time since the late 1960s (see table 8).

Readiness has nonetheless grown during the Reagan administration's tenure, though not by much.[3] "A rising tide lifted all boats," as it were. But now that the tide is receding, important boats, such as readiness, may be left on the shore to rot. It is therefore critical that an appropriate relationship between operation and support, and investment be preserved as overall defense spending is made more efficient.

In summary, then, the across-the-board Gramm-Rudman-Hollings mechanism for restraining defense expenditures is irrational and inefficient at best; at worst, its implementation could actually damage national security by slicing intolerable amounts from top-priority programs, rather than preserving them at the expense of low-priority ones. Gramm-Rudman-Hollings, however, is not the only threat to rational force planning. Even if the law is ruled unconstitutional, it will be critically important that reasonable priorities be established, and intelligent choices made, in formulating an alternative to the president's defense budget, which has already been rejected in Congress. In framing a responsible alternative, certain structural budget constraints (for example, large

3. CBO, "Defense Spending: What Has Been Accomplished," Staff Working Paper, April 1985, pp. 20, 29.

Table 7. Budget Authority Reductions Required for Alternative Outlay Growth Rates, Fiscal Years 1987–91

Millions of dollars

Item	1987	1988	1989	1990	1991	Total
Administration's budget authority plan[a]	311,600	332,400	353,500	374,700	395,500	1,767,700
Budget authority consistent with real outlay freeze[b]	274,809	293,301	306,777	316,807	324,191	1,515,885
Required reduction from administration plan	36,791	39,099	46,723	57,893	71,309	251,815
Budget authority consistent with 3 percent real outlay growth[b]	288,624	316,809	340,660	361,858	381,059	1,689,010
Required reduction from administration plan	22,976	15,591	12,840	12,842	14,441	78,690

a. Data from *Historical Tables, Budget of the United States Government, Fiscal Year 1987*, table 5.1.

b. The budget authority levels needed in order that outlays conform to the specified growth tracks are calculated using the equations presented in the appendix and five-year aggregate outlay rates, computed as specified there, of 0.56, 0.22, 0.11, 0.05, and 0.02. The computation of these aggregate outlay rates employs outlay rates for each individual appropriation title, from Department of Defense, *Financial Summary Tables, Fiscal Year 1987*, tab M. The calculation assumes no rescission of prior-year budget authority and no change in the mix among appropriation titles from the base year forward.

backlogs, due to differential defense outlay rates) must be appreciated. Having reviewed these, the way is clear for an examination of the inescapable question, "How much is enough?" The first step in answering it is to identify the basic objectives of U.S. defense policy; in other words to ask, "Enough for what?"

Basic National Security Requirements

For some time the fundamental goals of American national security policy have been relatively clear. In the conventional (nonnuclear) sphere, which accounts for the bulk of U.S. spending, the main missions are the defense of Western Europe, of the Persian Gulf, of South Korea, and of sea and air lanes to these theaters of war. To determine "how much is enough," these contingencies are examined in detail below.[4] It

4. While Europe, the Gulf, and Korea are the specific focal points of U.S. conventional force planning, larger alliance or regional security issues or both are presumed to be at stake. For example, the security of Saudi Arabia is of concern in the Persian Gulf though, for force planning and budgeting purposes, a Soviet invasion of Iran is the

Table 8. Ratio of Operation and Support Costs to Investment Costs, Fiscal Years 1971–80 and 1981–90[a]

Year	Ratio	Year	Ratio
1971	1.96	1981	1.56
1972	1.83	1982	1.35
1973	1.90	1983	1.21
1974	2.03	1984	1.18
1975	2.15	1985	1.11
1976	1.92	1986	1.10
1976T[b]	2.47	1987	1.13
1977	1.66	1988	1.11
1978	1.69	1989	1.10
1979	1.67	1990	1.09
1980	1.74	Average, 1981–90	1.19
Average, 1971–80	1.87		

Sources: Based on fiscal 1971–75 data from Office of the Assistant Secretary of Defense (Comptroller), *National Defense Budget Estimates for FY 1986* (DOD, 1985), pp. 85–86; and fiscal 1976–90 data from *Historical Tables, Budget of the United States Government, Fiscal Year 1987*, table 5.1.

a. Operation and support costs consist of appropriations for military personnel, operation and maintenance, and family housing. Investment costs consist of appropriations for procurement; research, development, test, and evaluation; and military construction. Figures are for Defense Department military functions (051 account).

b. Fiscal 1976 transition quarter (July through September).

does not suffice simply to compare Western inventories with those of the Soviets and their allies; some form of dynamic analysis taking into account the operational factors known to be crucial is necessary. This is equally the case in the nuclear arena; but there the effort has been complicated of late by fundamental ambiguities about goals.

Strategic Forces

For many years the deterrence of nuclear attack on the United States was indisputably the long-term top-priority goal of American defense policy. In his famous "Star Wars" speech in March 1983, President Reagan held out a rather different long-term goal: to render nuclear weapons "impotent and obsolete" through a dramatic expansion of research and development on strategic defenses. In the end, defense

dominant regional contingency. Similarly, the security of Japan is presumed to be enhanced by a strong U.S. military presence in northeast Asia, though the direct defense of South Korea is (like Iran) the most demanding and prominent of the planning contingencies.

would supplant deterrence; the promise of "assured survival" would displace the threat of "assured destruction."

As originally conceived, Strategic Defense Initiative (SDI) research would have experienced unprecedented average annual growth rates of more than 50 percent a year (nominal), with cumulative budget authority surpassing $25 billion by the beginning of fiscal 1990, by which point the SDI—narrowly defined to exclude defenses against Soviet bombers and cruise missiles launched from air and sea—would account for more than 15 percent of the Defense Department's total research and development effort.[5] Many billions would follow, as none of this research was to eventuate in a weapon of any kind.

Fiscal realities now demand what efficiency has long called for: a serious reconsideration of the pace at which the SDI is to be pursued.

Strategic Defense

One can imagine various defensive schemes emerging from the Strategic Defense Initiative. At one end of the spectrum would be a ground-based system designed to defend hardened targets in the continental United States (such as missile silos) by intercepting Soviet ballistic missile warheads after their reentry into the atmosphere (a so-called terminal point defense). At the other end of the spectrum would be a multilayered space- and ground-based system designed to attack Soviet ICBMs in each phase of their trajectory, and to defend against air-launched and sea-based nuclear threats, all supplemented by civil defenses, with extensions to allied territory. Costs of such a comprehensive strategic defense could run to trillions of dollars, while costs of a terminal defense against ballistic missiles might be as low as $50 billion; intermediate possibilities such as multilayered ballistic missile defenses without air- or sea-defense components have been estimated to cost in the $400–$800 billion range.[6]

Precise costs for the various levels of strategic defense are unknown, because even against a fixed threat, the sheer technological uncertainty

5. CBO, "Analysis of the Costs of the Administration's Strategic Defense Initiative: 1985–1989," Staff Working Paper, May 1984, table 2.

6. See Paul Stares and John Pike, "The 'Star Wars' Initiative: Problems and Prospects," *Space Policy*, vol. 1 (May 1985), p. 158. At such prices, anything approaching a comprehensive strategic defense would require draconian cuts in nonnuclear forces. Given the fiscal realities, the safety of a "defense-dominant world," if attained at the expense of conventional forces, can be seriously questioned.

is immense; and, of course, the threat is not fixed. Indeed, this is where all optimistic parallels to the Wright brothers, the Manhattan Project, or the U.S. manned lunar landing break down. Those were races against nature, not against a scientifically advanced adversary bent on overcoming an American program. Any assessment of cost and feasibility must take into account some plausible Soviet reactions.

For instance, it may be that an effective defense against ballistic missiles would require reductions in the adversary's offensive forces; indications, however, are that a deployment of strategic defenses would have the opposite effect. Defense Secretary Weinberger's own pre-summit letter to President Reagan supported this view, arguing that "even a probable [Soviet] territorial defense . . . would require us to increase the number of our offensive forces."[7] Saturation—overloading the system's capacity to sort out and destroy targets—is only one possible tactic against a strategic defense. Evasion is another.[8] The Soviets might also directly attack, or "blind," critical components of a space-based ballistic missile defense (in this respect, an agreement limiting further development and testing of antisatellite weapons could be central to any future defense). Add to this the fact that a true population defense can tolerate virtually no leakage, and the conclusions reached under the auspices of the Office of Technology Assessment are compelling:

> The prospect that emerging "Star Wars" technologies, when further developed, will provide a perfect or near-perfect defense system, literally removing from the hands of the Soviet Union the ability to do socially mortal damage to the United States with nuclear weapons, is so remote that it should not serve as the basis of public expectation or national policy about ballistic missile defense.[9]

Perfect *partial* defenses, against Soviet ICBMs, would provide no defense against Soviet sea- or air-launched cruise missiles or bombers.

7. Cited in Leslie H. Gelb, " 'Star Wars' Advances: The Plan vs. the Reality," *New York Times*, December 15, 1985. The possibility of the Soviets responding with offensive force increases was also explicitly recognized by Undersecretary of Defense Fred C. Iklé before a Senate Armed Services subcommittee. Walter Pincus, "Panel Told 'Star Wars' May Spark Increase in Soviet Offensive Forces," *Washington Post*, February 22, 1985.

8. For instance, the Defense Intelligence Agency has reportedly estimated that the Soviets could deploy a fast-burn booster by 1993 if they chose to. Fred Kaplan, "Snag Seen for 'Star Wars' Defense," *Boston Globe*, February 3, 1986.

9. Ashton B. Carter, *Directed Energy Missile Defense in Space, Background Paper*, prepared for the Office of Technology Assessment (Washington, D.C.: OTA, 1984), p. 81.

Indeed, the attempt to develop a defense against ballistic missiles seems less likely to put the nuclear genie back in the bottle than it is to let new genies out, accelerating the strategic competition at sea, requiring defensive initiatives there, efforts to counter these, and so on. In the end, after vast expenditures, something akin to the current strategic balance might be restored. But this hardly seems efficient.

In the worst case, serious instabilities could develop along the way. For instance, a conventional war in Europe might well last three months (see the discussion below), perhaps long enough for the U.S. Navy to seriously degrade the Soviet nuclear ballistic missile submarine force.[10] If, having done so, the United States, using the strategic forces programmed for the mid-1990s, were to launch a first strike against the *fixed* ICBM silos of the USSR, and follow-up with cruise missile strikes, there is a better-than-even chance that not many Soviet silos would survive. (See table 12 below.) The Soviet retaliation—involving perhaps 600 mobile ICBM launchers by the mid-1990s—could be ragged indeed. A U.S. strategic defense incapable of handling an all-out Soviet first strike might be able to "mop up" a ragged Soviet retaliatory strike. That situation, or the perception of it, could be destabilizing.

At this juncture, then, comprehensive strategic defense does not appear to be a realistic goal. Partial defenses, still extremely expensive, could be destabilizing at worst. At best, they could *enhance* deterrence. So, how much enhancement does deterrence require? Is not a steady moderate program of research and development sufficient to preserve this option? Or is the "enhancement of deterrence" a matter of extreme urgency, requiring unprecedented peacetime growth rates in research and development? The Reagan administration, in proclaiming a "window of vulnerability," has suggested that the enhancement of deterrence is urgent, and that the retaliatory capabilities inherent in America's strategic offensive forces—the ICBMs, submarine-launched ballistic missiles, and bombers—have somehow lost an important measure of deterrent power. On closer examination, what Mark Twain said of himself might well be said of the strategic deterrent: the reports of its

---

10. For unequivocal statements that Soviet ballistic missile submarines would be targets, see Adm. James D. Watkins, "The Maritime Strategy," in *The Maritime Strategy* (Annapolis, Md.: U.S. Naval Institute, 1986), pp. 9–12. For earlier press reports of this Navy objective, see Melissa Healy, "Lehman: We'll Sink Their Subs," *Defense Week*, vol. 6 (May 13, 1985), p. 18, and "War Game Sends Subs Surging," *Defense Week*, vol. 6 (September 3, 1985), p. 15.

Table 9. Effectiveness of a Soviet Strategic First Strike, Start of Fiscal Year 1986

| | U.S. pre-attack strategic nuclear forces | | | U.S. strategic forces surviving if attacked on: | | | | | |
| | | | | Day-to-day alert | | | Generated alert | | |
Item	ICBMs[a]	SLBMs[a]	Bombers[b]	ICBMs[c]	SLBMs[d]	Bombers[e]	ICBMs	SLBMs[f]	Bombers[f]
Launchers	1,023	640	297	260	367	89	260	512	238
Warheads	2,123	5,728	4,108	544	3,276	1,232	544	4,582	3,286
Deliverable in second strike	...	...	...	413	2,620	899	413	3,665	2,398
Assignment by target type:									
Hard strategic[g]	...	...	...	324	...	542	324	...	1,446
Soft strategic	...	...	...	89	385	357	89	1,250	952
Peripheral attack	...	...	...	...	400	...	...	460	...
General purpose forces	...	...	...	...	400	...	...	460	...
Transportation targets	...	...	...	...	400	...	...	460	...
Power plants	...	...	...	...	100	...	...	100	...
Urban-industrial targets	...	...	...	...	935[h]	...	...	935[h]	...

Note: ICBM = intercontinental ballistic missile; SLBM = submarine-launched ballistic missile.

a. Launcher data from *Department of Defense Annual Report to the Congress, Fiscal Year 1986*, p. 303. Warhead data from International Institute for Strategic Studies, *The Military Balance 1985–1986* (London: IISS, 1985), p. 158.

b. Launcher data from *Department of Defense Annual Report, Fiscal Year 1986*, p. 303; the B-1B is not included in this analysis. Loadings for FB-111s, B-52G penetrators, and B-52H penetrators from Congressional Budget Office (CBO), *Modernizing U.S. Strategic Offensive Forces: The Administration's Program and Alternatives* (GPO, 1983), p. 86. Loadings for the standoff variants from IISS, *Military Balance 1985–1986*, p. 159.

c. Surviving launchers are computed assuming the Soviet SS-18 mod 4 overall two-shot (cross-targeted) kill probability given in table 10. Surviving warheads are assumed to be distributed across surviving ICBM types according to their pre-attack proportions. Deliverable warheads are computed by multiplying availability × reliability × number surviving = 0.95 × 0.80 × 544 = 413, using the availability figure from CBO, *Modernizing*, p. 84, and the reliability figure from CBO, *Counterforce Issues for the U.S. Strategic Nuclear Forces* (GPO, 1978), p. 18.

d. Assumes alert rates from CBO, *Counterforce Issues*, p. 26. A reliability of 80 percent is applied to obtain deliverable warheads; CBO, *Retaliatory Issues for the U.S. Strategic Nuclear Forces* (GPO, 1978), p. 9.

e. For launchers, this analysis uses the 30 percent alert rate given in CBO, *Modernizing*, p. 100. To compute surviving warheads, pre-attack loadings are multiplied by 0.3, then summed. On deliverable warheads, CBO estimates the compound probability of reliable operation and penetration of Soviet air defenses as between 70 percent and 76 percent; the average, 73 percent, is assumed. CBO, *Retaliatory Issues*, p. 9.

f. For SLBMs and bombers the generated alert rate of 80 percent from CBO, *Counterforce Issues*, pp. 26, 28, is assumed; even though a 95 percent rate is given in CBO, *Modernizing*, pp. 100, 103–04. Surviving and deliverable warheads are computed as above, with 73 percent deliverable for bombers and 80 percent (reliability) deliverable for SLBMs.

g. Minuteman III and IIIA, air-launched cruise missiles (ALCMs), and gravity bombs are assigned to hard targets; Minuteman II, Titan, short-range attack missiles (SRAMs), and SLBM warheads are allocated to other targets.

h. Surviving and deliverable warheads are allocated to other targets.

death are greatly exaggerated. To understand the situation, imagine the worst case.

Strategic Offense

Suppose the Soviets executed a "perfect" first strike, catching U.S. strategic forces on day-to-day alert, destroying all American ICBMs, 70 percent of U.S. bombers, and more than 50 percent of U.S. submarines. More than 4,000 warheads, capable of destroying a wide range of hard and soft Soviet targets in a second strike, would still be available to the United States. Even assuming literally perfect Soviet air defenses against surviving U.S. bombers and cruise missiles, more than 2,500 submarine-launched ballistic missile (SLBM) warheads would be deliverable in a U.S. second strike, more than enough to decimate many hundreds of Soviet conventional and nuclear military targets, while holding in reserve enough destructive power to meet demanding criteria of assured destruction (see table 9). This is with no MX or Midgetman missiles, no Stealth bombers, no B-1 bombers, no Strategic Defense Initiative, no Trident II (D-5) submarine-launched ballistic missiles, none of America's roughly 7,000 theater nuclear weapons associated with NATO, and none of the nuclear weapons of Britain and France. These figures, in short, represent the very widest window of vulnerability that the most optimistic Soviet planner could possibly imagine. Perhaps it is understandable that the Soviets have not attempted to "jump through."

In fact, prudent Soviet planners could not count on catching U.S. forces on day-to-day alert. If the United States exploited the warning time that should be available during a conventional war or other crisis, the American bombers and submarines could be put on so-called generated alert. In that case, 80 percent of U.S. bombers and SLBMs could be available—more than 7,500 warheads—for a second strike, of which the United States would have high confidence of delivering more than 6,000 (see table 9). Of these, more than 3,500 would be SLBM warheads. According to the Central Intelligence Agency, "the Soviets still lack effective means to locate United States ballistic missile submarines at sea. . . . We do *not* believe there is *a realistic possibility* that the Soviets will be able to deploy in the 1990's a system that could pose *any significant threat* to United States SSBN's [nuclear ballistic missile submarines] on patrol."[11]

---

11. Statement of Lawrence K. Gershwin, *Soviet Strategic Force Developments,*

Table 10. Assumed Soviet ICBM Performance in Two-on-One Attacks against U.S. Silos of 2,000-Psi Hardness[a]

Soviet ICBM	Accuracy of attacking warhead (CEP, in nautical miles)[b]	Explosive yield (megatons)[c]	Overall two-shot kill probability[d]
SS-18 mod 4	0.135	0.50	0.74
SS-19 mod 3	0.150	0.55	0.70
1985 CIA reestimate	0.216	0.55	0.46

a. Assumes Soviets allocate two warheads per U.S. silo. U.S. silo hardness of 2,000 pounds per square inch (psi) is from CBO, *Modernizing*, p. 84.

b. Circular error probable (CEP) is the radius of a circle within which the warhead has a 50 percent probability of landing. CEP for the SS-18 mod 4 is from IISS, *The Military Balance 1985–1986*, p. 162; for the SS-19 mod 3, I assume the SS-19 follow-on estimate from CBO, *Modernizing*, p. 90; this imputes to the SS-19 mod 3 higher accuracy than is given it specifically (0.162 nautical miles) in IISS, *Military Balance 1985–1986*, p. 162. The CIA reestimated the SS-19 mod 3's accuracy downward in 1985. The figure is from Michael R. Gordon, "CIA Downgrades Estimate of SS-19 . . . Saying Missile Too Inaccurate for First Strike," *National Journal*, vol. 17 (July 20, 1985), p. 1692.

c. Yields are from IISS, *Military Balance 1985–1986*, p. 181.

d. Computed as $1 - (1 - TPK)^2$, where the terminal kill probability, TPK, equals the product of a weapon's reliability and single-shot kill probability, $SSPK$. $SSPK = 1 - 0.5^{(LR/CEP)^2}$, where the lethal radius, LR, is computed as a function of warhead yield and target hardness using the first formula given by Lynn Etheridge Davis and Warner R. Schilling, "All You Ever Wanted to Know about MIRV and ICBM Calculations but Were Not Cleared to Ask," *Journal of Conflict Resolution*, vol. 17 (June 1973), p. 213. The algorithm credits the Soviets with perfect cross-targeting so that reliability is maximized over the attack. Overall reliabilities of 80 percent are assumed, higher than the value of 75 percent given in CBO, *Counterforce Issues*, p. 16.

The "window" narrows further when one considers that the United States could—technically—launch its ICBMs on warning of a Soviet attack, adding more than 2,000 warheads to the retaliatory blow suffered by the USSR. While "launch-on-warning" is an extremely hazardous doctrine, no prudent Soviet planner can ignore the possibility. This uncertainty contributes to deterrence. Aside from the numerous uncertainties associated with U.S. operational behavior, the Soviets face technical uncertainties as well.[12]

Finally, even assuming Soviet ICBMs perform as currently estimated (see table 10), and that the United States chooses to "ride out" the Soviet attack, the prevailing assumption that the American ICBM force would be wiped out is simply not supported by the available evidence.

How vulnerable are current U.S. strategic forces to the current

Hearing before the Subcommittee on Strategic and Theater Nuclear Forces of the Senate Committee on Armed Services and the Subcommittee on Defense of the Senate Committee on Appropriations, 99 Cong. 1 sess. (GPO, 1986), p. 17. Emphasis added.

12. See, for example, Bruce W. Bennett, *How to Assess the Survivability of U.S. ICBMs*, R-2577-FF (Santa Monica, Calif.: Rand Corp., 1980).

strategic forces of the Soviet Union? Any point estimate is, of course, subject to considerable uncertainty; one can err on the side of conservatism by choosing, from the range of plausible estimates, those most favorable to the adversary. Even using the highest plausible estimates of Soviet missile accuracy, reliability, and yield, and the lowest plausible estimates of U.S. missile silo hardness, and assuming only day-to-day alert rates for U.S. bombers and nuclear missile submarines, the counterforce first-strike capabilities of the Soviet Union are considerably less imposing than is generally assumed. Soviet targeting considerations (that is, how to distribute efficiently the most-advanced ICBM warheads, the SS-18 mod 4 and SS-19 mod 3, over the U.S. strategic forces) complicate the real-world attack. But the analysis here assumes that the Soviets are able to allocate two warheads to each U.S. silo, maximizing the so-called probability of kill (see table 10).

Even after absorbing a well-executed Soviet first strike, current U.S. forces are capable of threatening a large number of diverse hard and soft Soviet targets, while withholding over 900 warheads for assured destruction of Soviet urban-industrial targets should American cities be struck (see table 9). The United States would emerge, that is, with options beyond the indiscriminate destruction of Soviet society.

Notice that, even on assumptions that consistently favor the USSR, the U.S. *ICBM* force in particular is *not* wiped out; about 25 percent of the launchers and roughly 26 percent of the warheads (more than 500) would survive. This finding, moreover, seems consistent with the congressional testimony of CIA officials responsible for the analysis of Soviet capability: "The Soviet capability today against Minuteman silos is substantial but not perfect by any means. . . . It is certainly not our intention to create the impression that the Soviets today could destroy all Minuteman silos, period. They could do a pretty good job against them."[13]

It is interesting to note, further, that if U.S. silos were reinforced to the same hardness as that imputed to many Soviet silos, the U.S. ICBM survival rate would be well above the 5 percent survival rate so often assumed in discussions of the nuclear balance (see table 11).

In the short term, hardening of U.S. silos might marginally prolong the life of the fixed-site land-based leg of the strategic nuclear triad. In a

13. Lawrence K. Gershwin quoted in Michael R. Gordon, "CIA Downgrades Estimate of Soviet SS-19 . . . Saying Missile Too Inaccurate for First Strike," *National Journal*, vol. 17 (July 20, 1985), p. 1693.

Table 11. **Performance of Soviet Advanced SS-18 and SS-19 ICBMs against 2,000- and 4,000-Psi Silos**[a]

Soviet ICBM and target silo hardness	Single-shot kill probability (SSPK)	Terminal kill probability	
		TPK(1)	TPK(2)
SS-18 mod 4 against:			
2,000 psi	0.61	0.49	0.74
4,000 psi	0.45	0.36	0.59
SS-19 mod 3 against:			
2,000 psi	0.56	0.45	0.70
4,000 psi	0.40	0.32	0.54
1985 CIA reestimate			
2,000 psi	0.33	0.26	0.46
4,000 psi	0.22	0.17	0.32

a. Probabilities calculated as in table 10, varying target hardness from 2,000 to 4,000 psi. The terminal, that is, overall, probability of kill for one shot, *TPK*(1), is the single-shot kill probability, *SSPK*, times reliability. For two shots the overall kill probability, *TPK*(2), is $1 - (1 - TPK(1))^2$.

long-term race against accuracy, however, hardening alone will lose, as projections of U.S. capabilities against hardened Soviet targets (such as ICBM silos) suggest (see table 12).[14]

Against Soviet targets hardened to withstand nuclear blast overpressures of 4,000 pounds per square inch (psi), two-shot kill probabilities are projected to exceed 95 percent; against 7,200-psi targets, the standard calculations yield two-shot kill probabilities of at least 90 percent. Even reducing the numbers in table 12 to account for less than 90 percent reliability, U.S. two-shot kill probabilities against hardened Soviet targets would still be high.

Within the class of weapons capable of destroying hard targets, a distinction is drawn between ballistic missiles, which can be delivered

14. Indeed, superhardening of U.S. silos (for example, to 50,000 pounds per square inch) will also lose. One can imagine the Soviets countering such a program by "un-MIRVing," or "defractionating," a portion of their advanced ICBM force to replace multiple warheads of submegaton yield with smaller numbers of high-yield multimegaton warheads. Yields of 2 or more megatons, if combined with MX-like accuracy (circular error probable of 0.05 nautical miles, which, eventually, the Soviets will achieve) and reliability of 90 percent, produce overall two-shot kill probabilities of at least 95 percent against 50,000-psi targets. Ten-megaton warheads with the same accuracy and reliability would have a 90 percent kill probability with only one shot. The MX accuracy figure (CEP of 0.05 nmi) is from CBO, *Modernizing U.S. Strategic Offensive Forces: The Administration's Program and Alternatives* (GPO, 1983), p. 84; reliability of 90 percent is from Theodore A. Postol, "The Trident and Strategic Stability," *Oceanus*, vol. 28 (Summer 1985), p. 51. Kill probabilities were computed by the same method used in tables 10 and 12.

Table 12. Performance of Projected U.S. Systems against Soviet Targets of Varying Hardness, Mid-1990s[a]

U.S. missile system	Accuracy of attacking warhead (CEP, in nautical miles)	Explosive yield (megatons)	Soviet target hardness[b]			
			4,000 psi		7,200 psi	
			TPK(1)	TPK(2)	TPK(1)	TPK(2)
MX	0.0500[c]	0.335[c]	0.87	0.98	0.80	0.96
Trident II (D-5)	0.0700[c]	0.475[c]	0.79	0.96	0.68	0.90
Pershing II	0.0243[d]	0.050[d]	0.88	0.99	0.84	0.97
SLCM (TLAM/N)	0.0500[c]	0.200[c]	0.81	0.97	0.71	0.92
GLCM	0.0162[e]	0.050[d]	0.90	0.99	0.90	0.99
ALCM	0.0500[c]	0.200[c]	0.81	0.97	0.71	0.92
Small ICBM (Midgetman)	0.0700[c]	0.475[c]	0.79	0.96	0.68	0.90

Note: SLCM (TLAM/N) = sea-launched cruise missile (Tomahawk nuclear land-attack); GLCM = ground-launched cruise missile; ALCM = air-launched cruise missile.

a. Probabilities calculated as in table 10, varying target hardness from 4,000 to 7,200 psi.

b. On the 4,000-psi figure, see CBO, *Modernizing,* pp. 18–19; 7,200 psi is the highest public estimate available, "Navy to Develop New Trident Warhead," *Aviation Week and Space Technology,* vol. 118 (January 17, 1983), p. 26.

c. CBO, *Modernizing,* pp. 84, 86. MX and D-5 reliabilities are projected to be 0.9; Theodore A. Postol, "The Trident and Strategic Stability," *Oceanus,* vol. 28 (Summer 1985), p. 51. This value is assumed for all systems projected above.

d. IISS, *Military Balance 1985–1986,* p. 158.

e. Thomas B. Cochran, William M. Arkin, and Milton M. Hoenig, *Nuclear Weapons Databook,* vol. 1: *U.S. Nuclear Forces and Capabilities* (Ballinger, 1984), p. 180.

promptly (and are therefore called "time-urgent" hard-target killers), and cruise missiles which, because they fly at subsonic speeds, may take hours to reach their targets. While hard-target kill capabilities are required, it is not clear why *time-urgent* hard-target kill capabilities beyond those already programmed should be needed. At the receiving end, moreover, these two types of counterforce capability—time-urgent and delayed—will be increasingly hard to distinguish as stealth technology is extended to cruise missiles, as planned in the advanced cruise missile (ACM) program. Indeed, if one measures "time urgency" as the interval from *detection* to impact (rather than as real flight time), cruise missiles may, in some applications, supersede ballistic missiles as time-urgent hard-target killers. The use of cruise missiles in such a capacity would, admittedly, force on the U.S. president (or his designated successors) a commitment to launch hours before impact; hours seem like a long time in peace. After perhaps three months of conventional war in Europe, during which delays due to "friction" have come to be expected, the flight time of a cruise missile might seem shorter.

In any event, given the U.S. strategic hard-target kill capabilities projected in table 12, and the possibility of a long conventional war in which many Soviet ballistic missile submarines could be lost, it is small wonder that the Soviets are deploying two mobile ICBMs, the SS-24 (rail mobile) and the SS-25 (road mobile). Whether the United States should follow suit, with the deployment of a $44 billion Midgetman, a small, mobile ICBM, is far from clear, for a number of reasons.

First and foremost is the basic question of need. The argument that the U.S. needs *time-urgent* second-strike hard-target kill capability beyond that to be provided by the submarine-launched Trident II (D-5) missile (and 50 land-based MX plus Minuteman IIIA missiles) remains to be made. Yet, all the Midgetman options under consideration are designed to provide this capability.[15]

Survivability is a second issue. The Midgetman ICBM is to be deployed on mobile launchers hardened to withstand overpressures of 30 psi, as they roam large dispersal areas in the United States. But how much area is enough? Without SALT II, or some other agreement, Soviet ICBM warheads could reach levels by the mid-1990s sufficient to barrage dispersal areas vastly larger than the 17,000 square nautical miles owned in the southwestern United States by the departments of Defense and Energy (see table 13).[16]

Evidently, as retired Lieutenant General Brent Scowcroft himself put it, in a March 1984 letter to President Reagan, "the cost effectiveness of the small missile will be heavily dependent on the existence of an arms control environment which would sharply restrict the number of [Soviet] warheads and throwweight."[17]

What can be said for some form of mobile Midgetman is that with arms control and with a sufficiently large parcel of land, it would extract

---

15. Donald A. Hicks, undersecretary of defense for research and engineering, has testified before the House Armed Services Subcommittee on Research and Development that 170 three-warhead Midgetmen, each weighing 75,000 pounds, would be as effective as the currently planned force of 500 single-warhead Midgetmen, each weighing 33,000 pounds. Hicks claimed that the heavier option would be $20 billion cheaper than the lighter version favored by the Air Force, which anticipates the possibility of slight weight growth (to 37,000 pounds) to permit the addition of penetration aids. See John J. Fialka, "Hot Debate on the Fate of Midgetman Missile Shapes Up in Congress," *Wall Street Journal*, March 4, 1986; Rowan Scarborough, "One-Headed Midgetman," *Defense Week*, vol. 7 (March 3, 1986), p. 10; and John Morrocco, "Perle: Single-Warhead ICBM a Waste of Funds," *Defense News*, February 24, 1986.

16. The 17,000 figure is from CBO, *Modernizing*, p. 72, citing an Office of Technology Assessment study.

17. Letter, Brent Scowcroft to President Ronald W. Reagan, March 21, 1984, p. 2.

Table 13. U.S. Operating Area Required to Ensure Specified Midgetman Survival Rates Assuming Unconstrained Soviet Forces, Mid-1990s

Square nautical miles unless otherwise specified

Projected Soviet growth	Number of Soviet ICBM warheads[a]	U.S. area required for missile survival rates of:[b]				
		10 percent	*30 percent*	*50 percent*	*70 percent*	*90 percent*
Moderate	10,632	23,627	30,377	42,528	70,880	212,640
Rapid	16,032	35,627	45,806	64,128	106,880	320,640

a. Al Tinajero and others, *U.S./Soviet Strategic Nuclear Forces: Potential Trends with or without SALT,* Congressional Research Service, Library of Congress, Report 84-174 F (October 5, 1984), pp. 62, 68.

b. For targets of hardness p between 10 and 100 psi, the lethal radius, R, of a weapon of yield Y_{KT} (in kilotons), detonated at its optimal height of burst, is $R(Y_{KT}) = (1685p^{-.620}) Y_{KT}^{1/3}$ meters. This formula was obtained by curve-fitting the overpressure results of Harold L. Brode and Stephen J. Speicher, *Air Blast from Nuclear Bursts—Analytic Approximations,* prepared for the Defense Nuclear Agency (Los Angeles: Pacific-Sierra Research Corp., 1985). The lethal area for such a weapon is $\pi[R(Y_{KT})]^2$. If a "packing factor" of 1.2 is used to ensure that circles overlap just enough to preclude a Midgetman's surviving, then the number of weapons N needed to cover an area A square nautical miles is (converting lethal radius to comparable units):

$$N = 0.46 \left(\frac{p^{1.24}}{Y_{KT}^{2/3}} \right) A.$$

Assuming a uniform random distribution, x percent of the Midgetmen die if x percent of A is covered, which requires x percent of N warheads. Assuming SS-18 yields of 500 kilotons and a 30-psi transporter, the operating area required to assure any specified level of survival reduces approximately to: (2 × number of Soviet warheads) ÷ (1 − specified survival probability).

from the Soviets a high "price to attack," forcing them to expend a large fraction of their land-based ICBM warheads in a first strike. While that fact might enhance crisis stability, it might also make the Midgetman missile's hard-target kill capability (which could reduce stability) superfluous, since the Russians would have evacuated most of their silos in order to mount the first strike. The hard targets remaining (residual Soviet silos and hardened command sites) could be covered by other means, notably Trident II (D-5s) and cruise missiles.

There is also something contradictory about the Reagan administration's apparent conviction that strategic defenses are feasible, and its plans to spend $44 billion on a mobile ICBM. If U.S. ICBMs can be defended, why should mobility be necessary?

Such questions, combined with the evident lack of consensus within the Pentagon on the Midgetman's design (and President Reagan's offer at Geneva to trade Midgetman away for a ban on mobile ICBMs) do little to impart a sense of coherence to the program. Given the outstanding additional question of need, or military utility, and the fact that the "window of vulnerability" was exaggerated to begin with, the case for literally *doubling* Midgetman funding, as requested for fiscal 1987, is unconvincing. Indeed, there is every reason to restrain funding sharply until a more coherent ICBM modernization plan is formulated. It is important that such a plan be developed, because the maintenance of a survivable land, sea, and air triad of strategic forces is worthwhile.

A survivable triad offers a hedge against Soviet technological breakthroughs that could reliably neutralize any one leg. Such a triad complicates Soviet planning for attack and for defense. It forces the Soviets to distribute offensive and defensive R&D over three types of American systems. And in a nuclear war, a Soviet strike on U.S. ICBMs (even if vulnerable) would provide warning to the bombers and vice versa.

In the long haul, however, the United States may have to entertain seriously the possibility that ICBM survivability and *time-urgent* responsiveness from the land-based leg may be incompatible, in a world of numerous, highly accurate high-yield warheads. In the end, survivable, time-urgent hard-target kill capabilities may have to be vested in the sea-based leg, with the ICBMs based in a way that provides high survivability, but at the expense of rapid response (for example, deep burial). What problems there may be in communicating with the submarines might well be solved at less than the estimated cost of Midgetman, for example. A serious study of that possibility seems overdue.

The Manned Bomber

Finally, the third leg of the triad deserves note; the basic question here is sometimes forgotten. In how many ways must the United States be able to penetrate Soviet air defenses with bombers and cruise missiles? With corridors through Soviet air defenses cut for it by submarine-launched ballistic missiles, such as the Trident I (C-4), the B-52 bomber (which is further equipped with its own nuclear-armed defense-suppression missile) can penetrate. Using the same tactic, or using its low radar profile, active electronic countermeasures, and nuclear short-range attack missile to shoot its way in, the B-1 bomber provides even higher confidence of penetration. Air-launched cruise missiles released from B-52s (or B-1s) outside of Soviet airspace, or cruise missiles launched from sea (the nuclear Tomahawk land-attack missile, TLAM/N) provide yet other, very high confidence, means of nuclear strike. In fact, in the CIA's estimation, "against a combined attack of penetrating bombers and cruise missiles, Soviet air defenses during the next 10 years probably

Table 14. Estimated Stealth Program Funding, Fiscal Years 1983–90

Millions of dollars of budget authority

			Program			
Year	Stealth bomber (ATB)	Advanced cruise missile (ACM)	ACM integration	Joint tactical missile system (JTACMS)	Small Stealth aircraft (F-19)	Total
1983	1,110	100	20	20	400	1,650
1984	1,325	400	25	150	500	2,400
1985	2,000	500	50	250	800	3,600
1986	2,405	670	125	300	900	4,400
1987	4,150	850	0	400	1,100	6,500
1988	4,760	790	0	450	1,200	7,200
1989	4,755	845	0	500	1,200	7,300
1990	5,400	200	0	500	1,200	7,300
Total	25,905	4,355	220	2,570	7,300	40,350

Source: Estimates from Joseph F. Campbell, "Stealth Bomber: Program on Track, Growth for Northrop," PaineWebber Status Report, February 13, 1986, p. 3.

would not be capable of inflicting sufficient losses to prevent large-scale damage to the U.S.S.R."[18]

Looking to the future, the application of stealth technology to cruise missiles, as envisioned in the advanced cruise missile (ACM) program, promises to increase yet further the already high confidence the United States enjoys. But while stealth technology, applied to cruise missiles and importantly to conventional forces, deserves strong support, the case for the Stealth manned penetrating strategic bomber (also called the ATB, for advanced technology bomber) has yet to be made, given the existing means of penetrating Soviet airspace, and particularly given the Stealth's estimated costs, shown in table 14.

Command and control arrangements for the use of Stealth bombers against Soviet mobile ICBMs (such as the SS-25) also raise concerns. The choice of nuclear targets, and the times and places of strategic nuclear employment, are decisions properly taken at high levels of national authority. Hence nuclear operations are governed by a system of positive control ("do *not* fire unless ordered to").[19] Stealth operations against Soviet mobile targets would, technically, be subject to the same

18. Statement of Gershwin, *Soviet Strategic Force Developments*, Hearing, p. 17.

19. This is in contrast to a system of negative control ("you may fire unless ordered *not* to").

system: the general location of a mobile target would first be determined by U.S. reconnaissance assets and conveyed (in real time) to national command authorities who, in turn, would transmit to the Stealth pilot the target's general location and the order to attack it. However, the pilot on the scene would then have to track down, precisely locate, identify, and release nuclear weapons against, the target on his own. A large amount of independent judgment would be involved. While the procedure would not represent a literal departure from positive control, it could require that the term be construed more broadly than it has been. This is disturbing to some.

Moreover, as a practical matter, the Soviets command huge expanses of territory over which to disperse such mobile targets, plus numerous avenues of concealment and deception to increase the already high level of positional/locational uncertainty that would be faced by an attacker, all of which call into question the feasibility of targeting Soviet mobiles.

If manned penetrators are necessary, further B-1s may be more cost-effective than Stealth bombers; they certainly appear to be cheaper.[20] While stealth technology R&D is worthy of funding through the advanced cruise missile and other programs, production funding for the Stealth bomber could be cancelled without jeopardizing the essential missions of the bomber/cruise missile leg of the strategic triad.

THE ABOVE judgments are reflected in the alterations to the administration's fiscal 1987–90 strategic nuclear force program recommended in table 23. Cancellation of production money and reductions in development funding for the Stealth bomber, the imposition of a cap of 50 on deployed MX missiles, reductions in the rate at which MX test missiles are procured, and real freezes (at fiscal 1985 levels) on SDI and Midgetman funding, account for most of the savings in budget authority, which total roughly $56 billion through fiscal 1990. Yearly reductions for these

---

20. PaineWebber estimates that "on a one to one basis, the stealth program will be about 25% more expensive than the B-1B, including extensive investment for composite tooling and autoclaves, offset by a somewhat less expensive avionics suite." In current dollars, PaineWebber estimates costs of $353.8 million per Stealth bomber and $283.0 million per B-1B. Joseph F. Campbell, "Stealth Bomber: Program on Track, Growth for Northrop," *PaineWebber Status Report*, February 13, 1986, p. 3. More recently, the B-1's manufacturer, Rockwell International Corporation, "offered to manufacture an additional 48 planes for $195 million each." Jack Cushman, "Rockwell Makes Bomber Offer," *Defense Week*, vol. 7 (March 24, 1986), p. 3.

and for the antisatellite and other stealth programs are given in table 23. Stealth technology is funded, though at levels lower and more sustainable than envisioned by the administration, whose plans for the Trident submarine, the Trident II (D-5) missile, and strategic command, control, and communications (C^3) are fully funded.

Conventional Forces

It is generally agreed that the most likely path to nuclear war is through a failure of conventional defenses. For this reason, and because nonnuclear forces—for the defense of Europe, of Korea, of the Persian Gulf, and of the air and sea lanes to these potential theaters of war— absorb the bulk of U.S. spending, conventional requirements must be assessed rigorously, by methods that go beyond the familiar static comparisons to account for critical dynamic factors. Nowhere have such operational dimensions been more cavalierly disregarded than in assessments of the Persian Gulf, a fact that makes that region an especially useful point of departure for this analysis of conventional contingencies, requirements, and budgetary alternatives.

Defense of the Persian Gulf

In the late 1870s, the Russians had recently annexed Merv, in what is now Soviet Central Asia, and the Russo-Turkish War was under way when—responding to fears in New Delhi of a Soviet threat to India— Lord Salisbury punned, "Mervousness would not stand the test of large-scale maps."[21]

A century later, the same might be said of the Persian Gulf. The Soviets share a border with Iran, and the number of Soviet divisions in the southern USSR exceeds, by a factor of more than three, the number of American divisions currently available to the U.S. Central Command, which is responsible for this region. The standard view of the situation can therefore be encapsulated as follows: They are near; we are far.

---

21. I thank Neville Brown for the exact quotation and for finally laying to rest all conjectures as to the source.

They are many; we are few. Hence, conventional defense is virtually infeasible.[22]

That view, however, is erroneous; for one thing, proximity in and of itself does not ensure access. Detailed maps reveal that between the Soviet Union and the oil fields of the Persian Gulf stand two formidable mountain ranges and an extremely limited, precarious, and vulnerable system of roads and rail lines. What is more, each side's wartime effectiveness (output) would depend on all sorts of operational factors such as warning and the readiness to act upon it, logistics, coordination, reconnaissance, flexibility, combat technology, and troop skill, none of which are evident in the raw numerical comparisons that typically pass for analysis.

Uncomplicated mathematical methods can capture these dominant dynamic factors and allow the force planner to analyze—in a conservative and plausible way—the relationship between inputs and outputs. For the Gulf, one can estimate, through careful modeling, how many divisions the Russians could support logistically in combat; how much delay the United States could impose on a Soviet invasion (by using airpower against transportation bottlenecks, or "choke points"); and how much force the United States could bring to bear (with airlift and sealift) in the time thus gained. Finally, one can simulate combat between U.S. and Soviet forces.[23]

What military requirements emerge when the Persian Gulf balance is assessed in this dynamic fashion? Reasonable people can disagree about how closely a given analysis approximates the ideal. But my attempt indicates that a modernized and well-supported Persian Gulf force of five tactical air wings (including an allowance for maintenance) and five divisions plus special forces (about four and a third armored division equivalents) should be able to cope with the range of plausible Soviet threats. This force would run in the range of $15 billion a year, as estimated in table 15.

The ground-attack air component of this force is capable of creating

22. Characteristic of this view, and of the static analysis underlying it, are the words of Edward Luttwak: "To consider the military balance in the Persian Gulf, with Iran as the possible theater of war, no computation is even needed: against a maximum of four or five American divisions that could eventually be deployed with great difficulties and greater risk, the Soviet Union could send 20 with great ease." Edward N. Luttwak, "Delusions of Soviet Weakness," *Commentary*, vol. 79 (January 1985), p. 34.

23. For detailed estimates and simulations, see Joshua M. Epstein, *Strategy and Force Planning: The Case of the Persian Gulf* (Brookings, forthcoming).

Table 15. Composition and Cost of U.S. Force Recommended for Defense of the Persian Gulf

Millions of fiscal 1986 dollars unless otherwise specified

Item	Fighter/ ground attack wings	Close air support wings	Armored division equivalents
Number of aircraft per unit[a]	130	130	. . .
Price per aircraft[b]	32	9	. . .
Unit capital cost	4,160	1,170	6,354[c]
Service life (years)	20[d]	20[d]	15
Operation and support (O&S) cost as percentage of capital cost	13[e]	27[e]	29[f]
Annual investment cost per unit[g]	416	117	847
Annual O&S cost per unit[h]	541	316	1,843
Annual cost per unit	957	433	2,690
Times: Number of units	3	2	4.29
Equals: Total annual costs	2,871	866	11,540
Annual grand total		15,277	

a. CBO, *Tactical Combat Forces of the United States Air Force: Issues and Alternatives* (CBO, 1985), p. 16.

b. Department of Defense, "Selected Acquisition Reports as of December 31, 1984," press release, April 9, 1985, and "Selected Acquisition Reports as of September 30, 1981," press release, undated.

c. Department of the Army, Office of the Comptroller of the Army, Directorate of Cost Analysis, *Army Force Planning Cost Handbook (AFPCH)* (DOA, 1982).

d. Department of the Air Force Regulation 173-13, "U.S. Air Force Cost and Planning Factors" (USAF, 1985).

e. Derived from O&S per squadron estimates in ibid.

f. Derived from Department of the Army, *Force Planning Cost Handbook.*

g. Assumes investment cost = capital cost ÷ ½ service life.

h. O&S cost = capital cost × O&S percentage.

four to six major choke points on each of the dozen major rail and road arteries from the USSR into Iran, while the ground and close air support components should be able to cope with the forces the Soviets could *actually sustain* in combat at the large distances from the USSR to the oil fields of the Gulf.[24]

A well-tailored force of this size is more efficient than the seven-and-a-third-division force approved by the Reagan administration, the main difference being the presence, in the latter case, of two superfluous light divisions. The highest U.S. priority should be to increase the speed of the force, through increased sealift, not its size; any U.S. response timely enough to make seven and a third divisions effective is timely enough to make five divisions sufficient.[25]

24. Ibid.
25. Ibid.

Two of the Army light divisions available to the U.S. Central Command (roughly 10,000 men each) should be disbanded; the personnel should be retained and reorganized as two independent brigades outfitted with tanks (for example, M60A3s) and other stockpiled heavy equipment appropriate for armored warfare in Europe. In the event of war, these brigades could be "rounded out" with existing National Guard or Reserve forces to form an additional division equivalent for NATO. The savings (roughly $900 million through fiscal 1990) from discontinuation of military construction activities associated with the light division at Fort Drum could be used to procure additional fast sealift for the newly created "round-out" division for NATO.

These recommendations—increased sealift (TAKRX ships) over acquisition of the C-17 aircraft, plus reductions at Fort Drum—are set forth in table 23. Their implementation alone would save $7.6 billion over the next four years. While increasing the efficiency of the U.S. conventional deterrent in the Persian Gulf, these changes would also enhance NATO's strength.

Defense of Europe

In Europe, further improvements can be made. Contrary to the prevailing view, however, the conventional military balance is far from hopeless. Not only is the general level of pessimism unwarranted militarily, it is counterproductive politically, compounding the effect of budgetary stringency to produce recurrent upsurges in anti-NATO sentiment, and suggestions that the United States reduce its commitment to European defense. While adjustments in the European-American division of labor are called for, the fundamental American interest in European security should not be a political or budgetary football.

The Primacy of NATO

Aside from the deterrence of direct attack on the United States, the defense of Western Europe is, and should remain, the centerpiece of American national security policy.

The United States has paid—in two world wars—an incalculable price for peace in Europe. Since World War II, Americans have run significant risks to make it secure. Cumulatively, trillions of dollars have been invested in Europe's postwar reconstruction and economic development. Sunk costs do not justify further expenditures, but they help to explain the "present value" of the asset. Today, Western Europe represents one of the largest concentrations of industrial and economic strength in the world. It also represents the largest concentration of political democracy in the industrialized world.

Were Europe to come under Soviet control, the global balance of economic, political, and military power would be revolutionized, and to America's detriment. Democracy, already quite rare, would be eradicated in Western Europe, as it was in Eastern Europe. And in the end, democracy in America could be imperiled as well—not necessarily by war, but by the enduring threat of it. Americans could be denied benefits of trade, and would certainly be denied all allied contributions to the common defense, which—though they should increase—are substantial. The political freedoms America seeks to preserve could vanish in the type of militarized social order that might be necessitated by unremitting long-term arms competition with an adversary controlling, as the Russians would, the preponderance of the world's advanced military-industrial capacity. America's power to reinforce allied and friendly states outside of Europe could be compromised, while the Soviets' capacity to threaten them would be increased.

America's formal alliance treaty commitment recognizes these interests, while the forward deployment of American ground troops ensures that the United States is *automatically* in conflict should forces of the Warsaw Pact threaten those interests by a military violation of the inter-German border.

We cannot be certain that, were Europe lost, things would evolve as disastrously as depicted above, but we cannot be sure that they would not. If the costs are bearable, we should pay them and avoid the risk. And the costs are bearable.

Feasibility of Conventional Defense

Indeed, the conventional military balance in Central Europe is considerably more favorable to NATO than is generally assumed. Portrayals of a hopelessly adverse conventional balance generally rest on static, simplistic, and often inconsistent assessments that fail to take account of operational, technological, and dynamic factors of critical importance.

The factor that traditionally dominates public debate about the military balance is sheer numbers. Simple numerical comparisons—"bean counts"—can be very misleading. For example, it is often noted that the *number* of Soviet divisions is greater than the *number* of U.S. divisions. But it is less often noted that Soviet and U.S. divisions are very different. A U.S. active division has almost 60 percent more manpower, is up to three times as expensive, and by the Army's own measures is about 50 percent more combat-effective, than its Soviet counterpart.[26]

The selective failure to credit quality is a related, and quite common, inconsistency. In general, when the U.S. military services frame their budgets, they want *quality*, but they tend to assess the Soviet threat as though sheer *quantity* mattered most. If numbers are the prime determinant of military power, then let us not spend so much on quality. And if quality is worth the money we spend on it, then let us not turn around and evaluate the military balance as though numerical ratios alone were reliable predictors of military outcomes; they are not.

Similarly, the United States spends billions of dollars on battlefield maintenance and support; on logistics and mobility; on training; and on command, control, communications, and intelligence (C³I). If the resulting levels of sustainability, personnel skill, and overall flexibility are worth what the United States invests in them, then their benefits should be reflected in assessments of the military balance. All too often, they are ignored.

Not only the pattern, but also the level of spending raises questions about the dominant view. Although the United States' allies can and should meet their spending growth commitments, the NATO alliance as a whole has consistently outspent the Warsaw Pact on defense since 1965, as shown in figure 1. The fiscal 1987 posture statement of the Joint Chiefs of Staff gives data showing the Western alliance continuing to outspend the Pact as of January 1, 1986.[27] A greater percentage of NATO's aggregate defense expenditure, moreover, is directed at the European theater. It is often forgotten that upwards of 15 percent of Soviet spending is directed at China.[28]

---

26. The manpower ratio is from General Accounting Office, *Defense Spending and Its Relationship to the Federal Budget* (GAO, 1983), p. 15; the cost ratio is from William W. Kaufmann, "Nonnuclear Deterrence," in John D. Steinbruner and Leon V. Sigal, eds., *Alliance Security: NATO and the No-First-Use Question* (Brookings, 1983), p. 56; the relative effectiveness in armored division equivalents (ADEs) is from William P. Mako, *U.S. Ground Forces and the Defense of Central Europe* (Brookings, 1983), pp. 114, 121.

27. Organization of the Joint Chiefs of Staff, *United States Military Posture for FY 1987*, p. 17.

28. Barry R. Posen and Stephen W. Van Evera, "Reagan Administration Defense

Figure 1. NATO versus Warsaw Pact Defense Expenditures, 1965–85

Billions of fiscal 1985 dollars

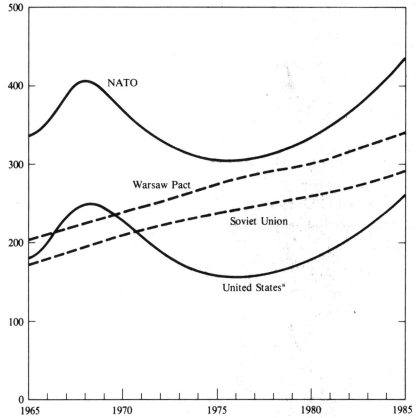

Source: Robert E. Foelber and Stephen Donahue, *Estimates of Soviet Defense Expenditures: Methodological Issues and Policy Implications,* Congressional Research Service, Library of Congress, Report 85-131 F (July 5, 1985), p. 100.

a. Excludes retired pay; includes Southeast Asia costs.

The prevailing view of the military balance in Europe is, nonetheless, that the Warsaw Pact is unequivocally superior at the conventional level. NATO puts more *in*, but the Warsaw Pact is assumed to get more *out* (in actual military capability). For that to be so, the Pact would have to be more efficient than NATO. There is no convincing evidence of this. Indeed, if the Soviet defense and civilian sectors are as intermingled as is often assumed (in, for example, defense cost estimates that include

Policy: Departure from Containment," in Kenneth A. Oye, Robert J. Lieber, and Donald Rothchild, eds., *Eagle Defiant: United States Foreign Policy in the 1980s* (Boston: Little, Brown, 1983), p. 73.

Soviet railroads), then defense must share at least some of the efficiency problems of its civilian Siamese twin. The counterargument has been voiced that relative efficiency is not decisive, since the Soviets face a wartime military task (offense) that is inherently easier than NATO's (defense), but there is little evidence to support this. Indeed, as good Clausewitzians, the Soviets surely recall the master's own dictum, "The defensive form of warfare is intrinsically stronger than the offensive."[29]

One advantage NATO as the defender enjoys is the opportunity to fight from prepared—even fortified—positions. By contrast, the attacker must come into the open, exposing himself to fire, in order to advance.

This is well known to the U.S. Army, whose own field manual makes the same point: a concealed defender has a significant advantage over an exposed attacker (see figure 2). Another defensive advantage is the chance to fight on familiar terrain, which in NATO's case would facilitate the channeling of Soviet armor onto some poor tank country, particularly if the terrain were prepared with "instant" antitank ditches and other cheap, effective modifications.[30] These terrain modifications can contribute to deterrence by denying the Soviets a quick win (see below) and by enhancing defensive advantages (for example, forcing the Soviets to stop and clear obstacles, exposing them to fire), without in any way "symbolizing the division of Germany." It would be well worth the additional four-year expenditure of about $400 million to undertake such "low-tech" but effective defensive preparations, as recommended in table 23.

Another advantage enjoyed by the United States is that its allies are

29. Carl von Clausewitz, *On War*, ed. and trans. Michael Howard and Peter Paret (Princeton University Press, 1976), p. 358.

30. "Instant" antitank ditches are segments of plastic pipe buried (at a depth of perhaps seven feet) in peacetime. In crisis, an explodable slurry or other liquid would be pumped in (it could also be pumped out if desired). Wartime detonation "would create an inverted 'V' tank ditch that at its deepest point would be about 12–15 feet, and at its widest point some 40 feet across," a serious obstacle for tanks. "Buried Explosive System Creates Tank Ditches Quickly," *Defense News*, February 17, 1986. A thousand kilometers of instant antitank ditching is estimated to cost $100 million (plus 5 percent a year in operation and support). The simple conversion of graded road shoulders into sharp concrete steps (and the emplacement of road dividers) would frustrate cross-road movement of armored forces. For another $100 million, 500 kilometers of road could be regraded, and so forth. Bridges and roads could be "prechambered" to accept enough charges to create 20,000 to 30,000 craters in war for roughly another $100 million (and 5 percent a year operation and support). On these and other approaches, see John C. F. Tillson IV, "The Forward Defense of Europe," *Military Review*, vol. 61 (May 1981), pp. 66–76.

Figure 2. Exposed Attacker versus Concealed Defender: Probability of First-Round Kill for a Soviet Sagger Antitank Guided Missile Shooting at a U.S. M60A1 Tank

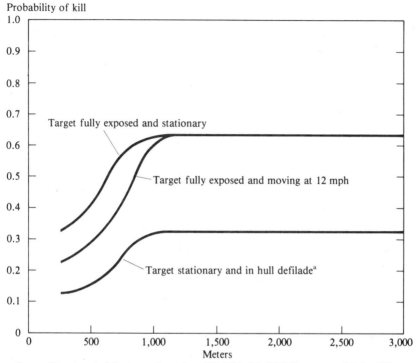

Probability of kill

Source: Department of the Army, *Operations,* FM 100-5, July 1976 (Government Printing Office, 1979), p. 3-13.

a. A tank is said to be in hull defilade position when its hull is inclined, hidden in the defile, with only its turret and main gun peeking over the top. In order to fire at ground targets, the tank's gun is at a depressed angle with respect to the tank's hull.

more reliable than those of the Soviets. Moreover, Western active units generally receive more training than Pact units (2.4:1 in the air).[31] And Western training is, in general, substantially more realistic; it draws upon more combat experience and upon the accumulated expertise of militarily skillful friends (for example, Israel). Finally, according to the Joint Chiefs of Staff, NATO enjoys a substantial technological lead in many critical areas.[32]

31. Joshua M. Epstein, *Measuring Military Power: The Soviet Air Threat to Europe* (Princeton University Press, 1984), p. 108.

32. Organization of the Joint Chiefs of Staff, *United States Military Posture for FY 1987*, p. 16. In fact, of the twenty basic technology areas listed by the Joint Chiefs of Staff, the Soviets are listed as superior in *none*.

The Air Balance

Historically, such qualitative factors have loomed larger than mere numbers in determining outcomes. Air-to-air combat is a prime example. In World War II, American pilots in the Pacific theater lost only one plane for every ten Japanese planes they shot down—an exchange ratio of 10:1. In the Middle East war of 1967 (the Six-Day War), the Israelis scored a ratio of 20:1; in the Yom Kippur War of 1973, the ratio was 40:1; in Lebanon, it was over 80:1. These disparities are explained by technological advantages and, above all, by differences in pilot skill. While it would be imprudent to assume Western performance at the high end of the above spectrum, it is unduly pessimistic to assume that the modest numerical disparities that exist should somehow nullify the West's superior, and far more extensive, training and its continuing technological lead.[33]

To this must be added a few further points. First, most of the Warsaw Pact's interceptors would not venture west of the inter-German border. They are limited in range and do not train for offensive operations. Second, penetration of NATO's airspace would expose Soviet attack planes to ground-based surface-to-air missile batteries that are almost never shown in the "air balance." In air warfare, as on the ground, the defender has some inherent advantages. For example, the defender of a high-priority target knows that the Soviet attacker will be *coming to him*, and can create (with electronics) the equivalent of terrain from behind which to ambush the "exposed" attacker. These advantages can be supplemented with traditional, proven, low-tech approaches to air defense, including increased sheltering for NATO's aircraft; runway hardening and repair; increased point defenses; improved deception and identification-friend-or-foe (IFF) capabilities; higher readiness and sortie rates so fewer aircraft are on the ground; and more flying and simulator hours to ensure greater combat effectiveness in the air.

Exploitation of these approaches (all of which are funded under the budgetary alternatives specified in table 23) should make the Soviet air threat manageable. Indeed, a case can be made that, despite important

---

33. On the historical record, see Epstein, *Measuring Military Power*, pp. 111–12. On the numerical balance, see CBO, *Tactical Combat Forces of the United States Air Force: Issues and Alternatives* (CBO, 1985), pp. 19–21.

strides since the mid-1960s, the Soviet air contribution to the conventional threat to Europe has been somewhat overrated to begin with.[34]

The Ground Balance

The NATO–Warsaw Pact ground balance depends on a large array of factors, one of the more basic being the attack option adopted by the Soviets.[35] For planning purposes, it is prudent to select the most challenging of these. This happens to be the one which, in my view, is most likely to meet the Soviet's chief operational wartime requirement: a quick win.

The reasons for a Soviet "short-war" doctrine are easily understood. Of course, no general or statesman, given a choice, would prefer a long war to a short one. But some military systems are distinctly less well adapted to lengthy conflicts. As an operational matter, a quick decision would circumvent Soviet problems of flexibility or sustainability that could prove telling in a prolonged war. A quick win nips uncertainty in the bud. It obviates the need for great flexibility by overwhelming the adversary before he can generate the unexpected counter, thus precluding any need to diverge from the predetermined plan or the routinized mission. The Soviets' operational shortcomings (inflexibility, difficulty in deviating from plans) should incline them to seek the earliest possible terminus, and to press their attack at an extremely high pace. Strategically, the Soviets would seek a decision before NATO has a chance to mobilize its superior industry. An attacker with potentially unreliable allies (for example, the Poles, Czechs, or perhaps East Germans) may seek a quick win lest they begin to defect. Finally, the Soviets might wish to press their attack at a ferocious pace to secure a decision before any of NATO's nuclear options could be executed.

Because of these imperatives, it is prudent to assume that the Soviets (a) would seek to maximize their mass (by mobilizing fully) and (b) would be willing to suffer very high levels of attrition in order to press the combat at a furious pace. The former assumption yields the NATO-Pact static balance ninety days after mobilization shown in table 16. The

34. See Epstein, *Measuring Military Power.*
35. For a number of Soviet attack options, see Mako, *U.S. Ground Forces,* pp. 40–48.

Table 16. NATO versus Pact Forces on the Central Front: M + 90 Static Conventional Balance[a]

Force	Division formations[b]	Armored division equivalents[b]	Weighted unit value[c]	Close air forces[d]
NATO				
United States	24	24⅛	1,149,258	...
United Kingdom	4	2½	118,725	...
France	12	3¾	180,462	...
West Germany	14	10½	498,645	...
Other	7	4¾	227,952	...
Total	61	45⅝	2,175,042	1,500
Warsaw Pact				
USSR	90	60¾	2,885,017.5	...
Non-Soviet	30	20¼	961,672.5	...
Total	120	81	3,846,690.0	1,600

a. M + 90 stands for mobilization day plus 90 days.

b. From Andrew Hamilton, "Redressing the Conventional Balance: NATO's Reserve Military Manpower," *International Security*, vol. 10 (Summer 1985), p. 116, citing estimates of William P. Mako, *U.S. Ground Forces and the Defense of Central Europe* (Brookings, 1983). Soviet and non-Soviet Warsaw Pact division formations are assumed to have equal ADE scores.

c. Computed by multiplying armored division equivalents by 47,490, the weighted unit value (WUV) of a standard U.S. armored division. Mako, *U.S. Ground Forces*, p. 114. WUV scores provide a common measure of lethality, or combat power, for U.S. and Soviet ground forces. The method was developed by the U.S. Army.

d. Sum of the phase I and phase II fixed-wing and helicopter close air support aircraft for NATO and the Pact, as estimated by Barry R. Posen, "Measuring the European Conventional Balance: Coping with Complexity in Threat Assessment," *International Security*, vol. 9 (Winter 1984–85), p. 72.

Soviets might attack earlier, but with far lower readiness and lethality; the prospects for tactical surprise are not good (and in no event is NATO's political responsiveness to warning an especially budget-sensitive issue).

The actual course of the war—who wins, how long the conflict lasts, how much territory is sacrificed—is highly uncertain but would clearly depend on a large number of factors not reflected in the static comparison of table 16. How many missions (sorties) a day might each side's close air support planes fly? What attrition rate per sortie might be suffered by each side? How many armored fighting vehicles could each side be expected to destroy on average per sortie? Would NATO extract ground-to-ground exchange ratios (attacker killed per defender killed) comparable to Israel's performance in the 1973 war (4.5:1)? Or at the other extreme, budgeters might assume that NATO-to-Pact divisional cost ratios have bought no comparable advantage in effectiveness (in which case the Soviets' divisions are more efficiently designed and the Americans' should change). In planning and budgeting, is the United States justified in presuming any of the advantages available to a prepared defender, or should planners treat it as axiomatic that NATO will be caught off-guard and subjected to surprise defeat (in which case more spending will not help)?

As a conservative gauge of material adequacy, it is possible to capture warfare's dominant dynamic factors.[36] The even-handed assignment of historically plausible values to such factors would not lead the Soviets to feel confident of a quick or easy victory over NATO. Indeed, conservative dynamic simulations suggest that NATO possesses the material wherewithal to stalemate the Warsaw Pact. They also show that wars of substantial duration are altogether plausible.

These points are substantiated in figure 3, whose solid and dotted curves simulate, respectively, two NATO–Warsaw Pact wars, each of which is consistent with the prewar static balance as measured in table 16 (that is, with NATO's initial combat power score at 2.2 million, and the Pact's at 3.8 million). The curves simulate—in an abstract but conservative way—the mutual attrition over time of NATO and Warsaw Pact forces, the salient point being that, in each case, NATO comes from behind to stalemate the initially larger force.[37]

Such assessments assume, of course, that NATO does not allow Soviet investments to go unanswered in the future, and that NATO maintains its forces in an adequate state of readiness, all of which is ensured under the budgetary recommendations offered in table 23. The assessment also assumes that NATO responds to warning of Soviet attack, mobilizes in a timely way, and is able adequately to sustain conventional operations. There is no material reason why NATO should fail to meet its basic requirements, especially if a U.S. heavy division equivalent were added, and a program of terrain modification and obstacle preparation were instituted, as proposed above.

Misallocations of resources, however, could compromise the effort. Moreover, strong conventional forces may in fact lower, not raise, the nuclear threshold if they are *applied* in escalatory ways. Two initiatives,

36. See Joshua M. Epstein, *The Calculus of Conventional War: Dynamic Analysis without Lanchester Theory* (Brookings, 1985).

37. Technically, since the curves cross, NATO "wins" in these simulations. But the absolute levels of attrition are sufficiently close to mutual annihilation that stalemate is the more conservative and appropriate term. In neither simulation does NATO lose ground.

Figure 3. NATO versus Pact Forces on the Central Front: The Dynamic Conventional Balance

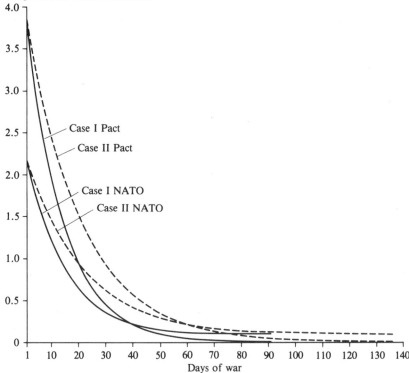

Ground lethality
(weighted unit value in millions)

Case I Pact

Case II Pact

Case I NATO

Case II NATO

Days of war

Sources: Simulations produced by applying the static numerical estimates of table 16, and other factors, in the dynamic model set forth in Joshua M. Epstein, *The Calculus of Conventional War: Dynamic Analysis without Lanchester Theory* (Brookings, 1985). The other factors employed (see *The Calculus* for complete definitions) are as follows: an average offense-defense ground-to-ground casualty-exchange ratio of 1.85 (far lower than divisional cost ratios and lower than traditional military offense-versus-prepared-defense planning factors of up to 3:1; see Barry R. Posen, "Measuring the European Conventional Balance: Coping with Complexity in Threat Assessment," *International Security*, vol. 9 [Winter 1984–85], pp. 51–52 note, 56, 80–81; and John J. Mearsheimer, "Why the Soviets Can't Win Quickly in Central Europe," *International Security*, vol. 7 [Summer 1982], pp. 15–16); a NATO withdrawal threshold ground attrition rate (in ADEs) of 6 percent a day; a maximum withdrawal rate of 20 kilometers a day (actual withdrawal rates are assumed to depend on the difference between actual attrition rates and the withdrawal threshold rate, here 6 percent); and a Pact equilibrium daily attrition rate of 7.5 percent.

These assumptions conservatively credit the Pact with the capacity to endure attrition rates higher than those NATO is willing to suffer before giving ground (7.5 versus 6 percent). By historical standards, these rates are very high; even so, a fight to the finish lasts three months. For historical rates, see Posen, "Measuring the European Conventional Balance," pp. 79–80. Thirty-three percent reductions in the Pact's equilibrium attrition rate (from 7.5 to 5 percent), in its opening prosecution rate (from 5 to 3.3 percent), and in NATO's withdrawal threshold (from 6 to 4.5 percent) would prolong the war by more than a month, to 136 days, as shown in case II. These are the only assumptions that differ from case I. Each side's close air attrition rate per sortie is 5 percent, high historically; armored fighting vehicles (AFVs) killed per NATO sortie is 0.5, and 0.25 for the Pact; 1,200 AFVs per division equivalent are assumed (see Posen, "Measuring the European Conventional Balance," pp. 72–73). NATO is assumed to average 3 sorties per day; the Pact, 2. For a discussion of comparative Soviet/Western strengths and weaknesses in the ground support of air operations, see Joshua M. Epstein, *Measuring Military Power: The Soviet Air Threat to Europe* (Princeton University Press, 1984), chaps. 2, 3.

the so-called deep-attack strategy—which is closely linked to emerging technologies (ET)—and the maritime strategy deserve scrutiny in both these respects.

Deep Attack and Emerging Technologies

It is widely believed that the Soviets and their allies would attack Western Europe in multidivisional waves, called echelons, supported by tactical aviation. The deep-attack strategy focuses on the delay, disruption, and destruction of the Soviets' reinforcing echelons, or "follow-on" forces, as they are known, and on the suppression of the Warsaw Pact's airfields. Conventionally armed ballistic missiles have been proposed in connection with the airfield-suppression mission. To the extent that it involves using conventionally armed ballistic missiles launched from NATO territory, deep attack could increase the escalatory pressures inherent in conventional war. The Soviets might find it hard to distinguish conventionally armed ballistic missiles from nuclear-armed ones in flight.

This may not be a pressing concern, since the Air Force prefers to perform this mission with penetrating aircraft. But it is an issue that could loom larger for NATO in the 1990s. The general efficiency of the deep-attack strategy, however, is an immediate issue.

For the reasons outlined above, the Soviets would seek a quick decision over NATO. NATO's top deterrent priority must be to make the Soviets' best bet (a quick win) look bad, not to make a bad bet (a long war involving numerous echelons) look worse. The deep-attack strategy (with which emerging technologies are closely associated) does the latter, but at the expense of missions, like close air support, that are essential to the former. And in the final analysis, if NATO cannot hold the Soviets' first echelon, retaliation on the second will be cold comfort. NATO's main effort should be concentrated on the front lines (called the forward edge of the battle area, or FEBA). The emerging surveillance, target-acquisition, and precision-guidance technologies now associated with deep attack might more profitably be focused there as well (rather than hundreds of kilometers to the east).

The forces of the Soviet second echelon, moreover, are not as combat-capable as those of the first echelon. In any event, they can be attacked more easily when they are close to the FEBA than when they are progressing toward it over Eastern Europe's dense and redundant transportation network, itself a target system whose suppression would require operations in hostile airspace and the further diversion of resources from the vital task of thwarting the Soviets' first echelon.

The Soviets, furthermore, may be able to circumvent the ground component of the strategy (follow-on force attack, or FOFA), by sacrificing surprise, deploying all the "follow-on" forces forward, and building up to maximum mass before attacking NATO, as in the simulations in figure 3.

NATO air superiority is to be attained primarily through suppression of Soviet airfields far behind enemy lines. The very demanding deep penetration of enemy airspace by piloted aircraft (notably, the F-15E) is envisioned. This mission, if not supplanted by them, should be supplemented with the more traditional and proven defensive approaches to air supremacy noted above.

All this leaves aside the important question of whether the emerging technologies themselves can be countered (for example, inexpensively spoofed). As a subsidiary point, the strategy places some reliance on joint (interservice cooperative) programs, such as JSTARS (Joint Surveillance and Target Acquisition Radar System) when, traditionally, joint programs have been ill-starred.

It is critical that NATO preserve its technological lead over the Warsaw Pact. A level of emerging-technology research and development consistent with that goal should be sustained. A balanced approach stressing the front lines of NATO's defense is called for, not a headlong plunge into promising, but unproven, longer-range technologies.

This judgment is reflected in the cancellations and deferrals of emerging-technology programs recommended in the Army/Air Force section of table 23. Those actions would save roughly $7.7 billion in budget authority over four years. Also consistent with the above discussions of the air balance and NATO's strategy, the ground-attack variant of the F-15 aircraft—the F-15E—which is closely associated with the deep-attack strategy, is terminated, while purchases of the less-expensive, multipurpose F-16 are increased, and the F-4 is upgraded, as the Air Force modernizes and expands. These changes would save $9.6 billion over fiscal 1987–90. F-16 growth, when supplemented by an expansion in airbase-survivability programs, would compensate for a reduction in the rate of growth of the Patriot (surface-to-air missile) air defense program. The net effect of these changes would be to cut $1.3 billion from defense. The adoption of all these recommendations would save nearly $19 billion in budget authority over four years, as broken down in table 23.

The Maritime Strategy

Another offensively oriented initiative that, like deep attack, is both inefficient and potentially escalatory is the so-called maritime strategy, which provides the doctrinal underpinnings of the fifteen-carrier, 600-ship Navy planned by the Reagan administration.

In a war, the Soviets—for a variety of political, strategic, and operational reasons—would place a premium on securing a quick conventional victory over NATO. It is critical to deterrence, therefore, that the Russians be convinced that NATO cannot be defeated quickly and will convert the conflict into a long war in which its superior industrial power will be brought to bear. Navies contribute to this long-war capability.

For the Western alliance to sustain conventional land and air operations for more than a few months the U.S. Navy would have to protect NATO's sea line of communication (SLOC) from Soviet bombers and submarines. But this primary naval objective might be achieved in either one of two ways: defensively or offensively. The former tactic calls for the Navy to concentrate its defenses near the gaps that separate Greenland, Iceland, and the United Kingdom (the so-called GIUK gaps), there to lie in wait for the Soviets, forcing them to run a series of defensive gauntlets before engaging U.S. carriers and Europe-bound convoys. The alternative tactic would be to assemble a large-scale offensive naval strike force and steam north of the GIUK, north of Norway, and around the North Cape to smash the Soviet threat in its lair, Murmansk. The Reagan administration's support for the latter, offensive approach is clear.

How would a fifteen-carrier fleet be likely to fare in offensive operations against the Soviet Northern (or Pacific) Fleet? Here again one is dealing with a *specific* campaign, the feasibility of which cannot be gauged by any mere comparison of U.S. and Soviet inventories; a dynamic analysis, capturing the dominant (and highly asymmetrical) factors, is essential. Such an analysis shows that, in fact, a fifteen-carrier fleet would stand little chance of success in conducting offensive operations in these high-threat areas.[38] Specifically, even on assumptions

38. The analytic framework is set forth in Joshua M. Epstein, "The Great Naval

that are uniformly favorable to the U.S. Navy—best-case assumptions—a fleet of more than twenty carrier battle groups would be required to execute such operations while also fulfilling assignments in the Mediterranean, the Indian Ocean, and the Atlantic. At an estimated $18 billion per carrier battle group, such a fleet would cost roughly $90 billion more than the already terribly expensive fifteen-carrier, 600-ship Navy.[39]

There is no reason to assume this financial burden. If the Navy secures the sea lanes defensively—exploiting land-based airpower, mining, and antisubmarine warfare in the GIUK gaps—the case for even a fifteen-carrier fleet fades away; twelve carrier battle groups more than suffice.

The fifteen-carrier fleet therefore falls between two stools. If the Navy seriously intends to employ aircraft carriers offensively, a fifteen-carrier fleet is not nearly big enough; we should face the fact that at least five more carrier battle groups, and perhaps $90 billion more in defense spending, would be required. To safeguard the sea lanes, however, it is unnecessary to employ carriers in this fashion; defensive carrier employment is equally effective at lower cost. If the United States uses the latter, far more efficient approach, a twelve-carrier fleet is more than enough.

Associated with the maritime strategy's offensive surface naval actions are offensive undersea operations that would put Soviet nuclear ballistic missile submarines (SSBNs) at risk. There is every reason to believe this conventional counterforce campaign would be undertaken intentionally, as a deliberate attempt to degrade the Soviets' strategic retaliatory capability by conventional means.[40]

As Barry Posen has written, "a deliberate conventional campaign against Soviet SSBNs could be understood by the Soviets as the beginning of a damage-limiting strategic first-strike. Given the importance of nuclear weapons and nuclear war in Soviet doctrine, even the appearance of such a campaign could trigger dire consequences. American leaders may be surprised by the Soviet response, since they seem

---

Shoot-Out at Murmansk: Implications for the Fifteen-Carrier Fleet," unpublished paper, September 1982.

39. The $18 billion is capital cost only and includes prices for cruisers, destroyers, frigates, underway-replenishment ships, submarine escorts, and tactical aircraft. See CBO, *Costs of Expanding and Modernizing the Navy's Carrier-Based Air Forces* (CBO, 1982); CBO, *Future Budget Requirements for the 600-Ship Navy* (CBO, 1985); unofficial historical data provided by CBO; and Department of Defense, "Selected Acquisition Reports as of June 30, 1985," press release, undated.

40. Watkins, "Maritime Strategy," pp. 9–12.

to believe that so long as nuclear weapons have not been *used* in destroying Soviet strategic forces, the prospect of Soviet escalation is not raised."[41] In fact, that prospect might be raised very sharply; if so, the aircraft carriers themselves would make lucrative targets for Soviet nuclear response. As Bernard Brodie put it, "what better targets are there for such [tactical nuclear] weapons than our nice, big aircraft carriers."[42]

Surely, it makes no strategic sense to field large and expensive conventional forces in order to avoid nuclear war and then to apply those forces in ways that unduly risk stimulating nuclear escalation. Whatever else it may be, the maritime strategy involves offensive aircraft carrier operations against the Soviet Union and offensive submarine operations that would directly threaten Soviet strategic forces. Neither mission is necessary to defend the sea lanes and ensure the reinforcement of NATO (a critical mission). The undersea operation could prove highly provocative. Both are extremely expensive.

Some maritime advocates argue that the aim of the subsurface offensives is to force the Soviets onto a defensive posture from which they cannot threaten the sea lines of communication. But where is the analysis showing (a) that it is cheaper to defend the sea lanes this way and (b) that these alleged conventional war benefits outweigh the avoidable nuclear risks? Nowhere.

Parallel arguments are offered to support offensive U.S. aircraft carrier operations against Soviet forces in the north. But if the cost of tying down Soviet air forces in the north with U.S. battle groups is three or four times the price of defeating those forces using land-based aircraft in NATO's center region, then the approach is, again, inefficient. More to the point, can the Navy be sure the Soviets would in fact be tied down at all? Perhaps it is the United States that has been lured into allocating vast sums on long-war, and horizontal-counteroffensive, naval capabilities when the main Soviet objective would be a short land war focused on Germany.

On the basic conventional vulnerability of aircraft carriers, the Navy sometimes argues that it would only send carriers against the Kola

---

41. Barry R. Posen, "Inadvertent Nuclear War? Escalation and NATO's Northern Flank," *International Security*, vol. 7 (Fall 1982), p. 43. Emphasis added.

42. Letter, Bernard Brodie to Adm. Stansfield Turner, January 16, 1976, as quoted in Desmond Ball, "Nuclear War at Sea," *International Security*, vol. 10 (Winter 1985–86), p. 8.

Peninsula—home of the Soviet Northern Fleet—after Soviet naval aviation had suffered severe attrition. With what weapons is this severe attrition accomplished? Why not apply more of those weapons (for example, conventional cruise missiles) and finish the job, rather than investing tens of billions to be able to finish it with carriers? (Of course, any set of assumptions that makes carrier offensives against the Kola Peninsula appear feasible will make carrier operations south of the GIUK look easy by comparison.)

Sometimes the reinforcement of Norway (which fields a tough defense of its own) is offered as a justification for the maritime strategy. Why one must threaten the strategic second-strike capabilities of the Soviet state (that is, Soviet nuclear ballistic missile submarines) to reinforce Norway has yet to be established. Neither is it necessary to land Marines on the Kola Peninsula and outflank a Soviet overland threat to Norway. The terrain facing a Soviet land attack is formidable. The transportation system is sparse and vulnerable (bridges can be prechambered to accept explosives in crisis) and offers great leverage to a skillful defender, as the Finns proved to the Russians in the Winter War of 1939. The Soviet amphibious threat to Norway, in turn, can be addressed by the Norwegian navy, defensive mining, and shore-based airpower and artillery, while the Soviet air threat can be met with land-based aircraft from upgraded Norwegian fields (with a U.S. reinforcement from Scotland or the south Norwegian Sea if necessary).

Finally, third world peacetime contingencies and "showing the flag"—peacetime presence—are given as rationales for the maritime strategy. But under the current budgetary constraints, the burden of proof is on the Navy to articulate (a) the number of *simultaneous* peacetime presence missions for which the United States should plan, and (b) why a fleet of twelve carrier battle groups (and four surface action groups) should be inadequate to the task.

The dominant issue, however, is the maritime strategy's contribution to conventional defense in the big contingencies, notably the conventional defense of NATO. And in that connection the basic point is that if NATO loses the short war (which the Soviets plan for), then long-war capabilities—of which navies are the exemplar—will be pointless. In effect, the maritime strategy represents a massive diversion of resources from the immediate defense of Western Europe and into offensive surface and subsurface naval actions that are grossly inefficient in accomplishing essential naval tasks (for example, the defense of sea lanes), and which could prove escalatory in addition. Under current budgetary constraints, it is high time to abandon this risky and expensive approach.

Doing so would involve the transfer of three carriers into the Reserve and commensurate reductions in the growth rates of Aegis cruisers (CG-47s), Arleigh Burke–class destroyers (DDG-51s), auxiliary ships (for example, fleet oilers), subsurface escorts, and carrier-based tactical airpower (F-14s, F/A-18s, A-6s, and SH-60s). These measures, combined with the denial of procurement funding for the SSN-21 nuclear attack submarine and a slowdown in the procurement of SSN-688 submarines, would produce savings of nearly $41 billion over four years, as broken down by program and year in the Navy section of table 23.

The allies can and should meet their spending growth commitments. If they do so, and if U.S. defense spending is efficient, the Soviets should have little basis for confidence of a quick conventional victory over NATO. The alliance's conventional forces, backed up by theater nuclear and strategic nuclear forces, will present the Soviets with the most powerful overall deterrent that has ever existed, and should obviate the need for any fundamental revision in NATO's current strategy of forward defense and flexible response.

Execution of core conventional missions does require adequate means to sustain combat, and powerful naval forces, all of which can be provided while reducing unnecessary expenditures. The issue of sustainability, which has received much attention recently, requires a brief discussion of its own, particularly as it bears on the acquisition of modern precision ordnance.

Sustainability and Modern Munitions

Everyone supports sustainability, but few are willing to measure it with much care, or to venture an estimate of how much should be purchased as against other necessities. In general, sustainability is measured in days; one speaks of the need to sustain combat for 30, 60, or 90 days. Rules of thumb are widely applied to generate required stockpiles of ammunition. As an illustration, if each of 30 divisions consumes 1,000 tons a day, and it will take 60 days for stateside production to tool up to meet wartime demands, one had better stockpile on the order of $30 \times 1,000 \times 60 = 1.8$ million tons of ammunition in peacetime. The daily tonnage requirements come from assumptions concerning rates of fire. For artillery, one assumes a daily firing rate per tube (for example, 150 rounds per day), and multiplies by the number of tubes per theater (perhaps 5,000 for NATO Center) to generate this indirect, or area fire, ordnance requirement per day.

For modern precision-guided munitions, some costing more than $250,000 a shot, these level-of-effort methods are inappropriate. With advanced direct fire ordnance, a fixed daily firing rate is misleading. One should estimate needs in targets, not days.

For instance, how many ground targets (tanks and other armored fighting vehicles) would NATO confront in a large-scale Warsaw Pact attack? At roughly 1,200 armored fighting vehicles per division equivalent,[43] a 90-division-equivalent Pact attack presents NATO with 108,000 "threat" targets on the ground (assuming, conservatively, a literal fight to the finish).

Over the full panoply of NATO surface-to-surface and air-to-ground precision-guided munitions, tank rounds (such as high-explosive antitank and depleted uranium rods), and close air support gun bursts (at 40 rounds of 30mm ammunition per burst), the number of direct fire "shots" available to NATO for each of these 108,000 Pact ground targets is about 20.[44]

If "smart" weapons do not work, the United States should stop buying them. But if they work half as well as the services claim (when requesting funds for these weapons), then there is no reason why an allowance of 20 direct shots per ground target should be inadequate.

In fact, 20 shots assumes only one load of ammunition is available per tank; this is unrealistically conservative, since reloading is to be expected.[45] Moreover, for two-thirds of the 108,000 threat targets these shots are overdesigned. Only the 30,000 or so targets that are tanks are

43. Barry R. Posen, "Measuring the European Conventional Balance: Coping with Complexity in Threat Assessment," *International Security*, vol. 9 (Winter 1984–85), p. 73.

44. Derived by adding NATO's 480,000 tank rounds (12,000 mobilized NATO tanks at a single 40-round load per tank); 600,000 antitank guided missiles (400,000 U.S. and allied TOW plus 200,000 U.S. and allied Milan and Dragon); 50,000 air-to-surface precision-guided munitions; and a million close air "shots" (at 40 rounds of 30mm GAU 8 ordnance per shot), for a total of 2,130,000 direct fire shots, and dividing by the 108,000 Pact threat targets. Unofficial historical data provided by CBO; and Department of Defense, *Procurement Programs (P-1), Department of Defense Budget for Fiscal Year 1987* (DOD, 1986). See also "Pentagon Budget for Ammunition Called Excessive," *Washington Post*, September 24, 1985. I thank Barry R. Posen for very illuminating discussions of this issue.

45. With laser ranging, moreover, 105mm tank rounds probably deserve to be counted as well; they are excluded.

hard enough to require specialized shots. The remainder are armored personnel carriers and other soft vehicles that are vulnerable to indirect fire weaponry not counted above.

These indirect fire weapons include mortar, mines, and artillery; the last comprises around 9 million rounds of 155mm high-explosive and cluster munitions. Artillery can immobilize or destroy soft vehicles and can channel harder targets into zones designed to maximize direct fire effects. The Multiple Launch Rocket System (MLRS) and large stockpiles of iron bombs (for example, Rockeye) should be counted in addition. Seldom are the effects of indirect fire weapons included in deriving direct fire requirements.

Stockages of modern direct fire munitions should grow. But given existing stockpiles, it is hard to see why continuing the acquisition of modern munitions at the current rate should put sustainability—measured reasonably—in jeopardy. Denying an *acceleration* in the acquisition of modern munitions would save about $7 billion over fiscal 1987–90 (see the sustainability section of table 23). In this connection, there is ample reason to cancel the troubled advanced medium-range air-to-air missile (AMRAAM), which is now two years behind schedule, and whose costs have tripled, without achieving its performance goals.[46] Together these measures would yield four-year savings of $11.2 billion in budget authority.

Adopting a Current Services Approach to Selected Supporting Functions

Like sustainability, readiness gets a good deal more publicity than it does serious study; the common identification of operation and maintenance spending with readiness is especially suspect. Within the operation and maintenance (O&M) account, there are certainly functions directly related to the immediate combat capability of U.S. forces (for example, training for combat pilots and ground crews). But there are also activities of a "housekeeping" nature whose connection to the actual war-fighting power of the force is remote (such as routine property maintenance of military reservations in the United States). While important, there is no reason why the maintenance of these housekeeping functions at a current

---

46. CBO, *Reducing the Deficit: Spending and Revenue Options* (GPO, 1986), pp. 46–47.

Table 17. Savings from a Real Freeze on Housekeeping Funds in Operation and Maintenance, Fiscal Years 1987–90[a]

Billions of dollars

Item	1987	1988	1989	1990	Total
Savings in budget authority	2.9	3.8	5.1	6.6	18.4
Savings in outlays	2.1	3.4	4.6	6.0	16.1

Sources: Computed using budget authority data from *Historical Tables, Budget of the United States Government, Fiscal Year 1987*, table 5.1, and outlay rates from Department of Defense, *Financial Summary Tables, Fiscal Year 1987*, tab M.

a. Imposes a real freeze on 33 percent of operation and maintenance.

services level should jeopardize the real combat capability of the force. These areas of operation and maintenance, in other words, could be frozen in real terms without detriment to our security. Perhaps a third of the operation and maintenance budget falls into this category.[47] Savings from a freeze in these areas are estimated in table 17.

Combined with all the investment-slowing proposals set forth in table 23, this would still allow the ratio of operation and support to investment spending to rise over the levels proposed by the Reagan administration; if anything, combat readiness should grow as a result.

Rescission

Technically, large current-year reductions in outlays are possible through the rescission of budget authority granted in prior years. There is no reason why Congress should not institute the priorities outlined above for fiscal 1987 through 1990 retroactively to unexpended budget authority granted in fiscal 1984–86. Doing so would eventuate in rescissions totaling $18.8 billion (in budget authority) and maximum (that is, without cancellation costs) outlay savings of roughly $9.1 billion by 1990. (See table 18.)

In practice, cancellation costs would be incurred, since most of the monies rescinded would have been already committed to contract, or obligated. In fact, monies are "locked into" contract (obligated) much faster than they are spent, in part to deter rescission, a tactic that has been rather successful politically. Indeed, even Gramm-Rudman-Holl-

47. For example, the sum of real property maintenance; administration; other; base operation support; recruiting, advertising, and examining; and other logistics account for about 40 percent of the O&M budget. Thirty-three percent thus seems conservative. Office of the Secretary of Defense, *Operation and Maintenance Overview, Fiscal Year 1986* (DOD, 1985), p. 4.

Table 18. Outlay Reductions through Rescission of Budget Authority Appropriated in Fiscal Years 1984–86

Billions of dollars

Item	1987	1988	1989	1990	Total
Outlay reduction from rescission of:					
$4.2 billion in 1984 budget authority	0.4	0.2	0	0	0.6
$5.3 billion in 1985 budget authority	1.1	0.5	0.3	0	1.9
$9.3 billion in 1986 budget authority	3.2	2.0	0.9	0.5	6.6
Outlay savings					
Assuming zero cancellation costs	4.7	2.7	1.2	0.5	9.1
Assuming 15 percent termination factor	4.0	2.3	1.0	0.4	7.7

Sources: Computed using budget authority data from *Department of Defense Annual Report to the Congress, Fiscal Year 1985; Fiscal Year 1986;* and *Fiscal Year 1987;* and aggregate outlay rates for the investment accounts derived as specified in the appendix from data in Department of Defense, *Financial Summary Tables, Fiscal Year 1987,* tab M. Those aggregate outlay rates are, by year, 0.24, 0.34, 0.21, 0.10, and 0.05. The budget authority rescission estimates assume retroactive institution of the actions proposed in table 23 for the SSN-688 submarine, small ICBM (Midgetman), C-17 aircraft, Patriot missile, M2 fighting vehicle, Strategic Defense Initiative, antisatellite (ASAT) program, Army helicopter improvement program (AHIP), and AMRAAM (advanced medium-range air-to-air missile), plus cancellation of the V-22 aircraft, of battleship reactivations, and of 29 F-14 aircraft and 20 F-18 aircraft (extending the reductions of table 23 to two complete wings). No budget authority for the M1 tank is rescinded. The 15 percent cost factor is an estimate considered conservative by government officials interviewed by the author. The true value could vary considerably (a) between systems and (b) depending on where, in its funding, any particular system might be when affected.

ings exempts *obligated* prior-year monies from its automatic reductions for this reason. Of course, in avoiding the Gramm-Rudman-Hollings trigger, these monies are fair game. Procurement provides a good example of the obligation/outlay relationship.

Table 19 shows how legislators can be "for defense" without being "for the deficit"; out of every procurement dollar appropriated, the deficit increases by only 15 cents in the first year. But in that year, contracts will be signed which obligate the Department of Defense to spend 70 cents; 15 percent is spent but 70 percent is obligated. This is how big projects get their "noses under the tent" and then prove hard to stop.

Difficult though it may be to resist the tyranny of sunk costs, it is still vastly more efficient to rescind, even paying cancellation fees, than to saddle the budget with unnecessary life-cycle costs orders of magnitude larger. Doing so would result in the savings estimated in table 18.

Prices

Thus far, the discussion has concerned force structure. And in fact the largest efficiencies in defense are to be made at the level of force

Table 19. The "Nose-under-the-Tent" Phenomenon of Fast Obligations and Slow Outlays: The Case of Procurement

Percent of first-year budget authority

	Year					
Item	*First*	*Second*	*Third*	*Fourth*	*Fifth*	*Sixth*
Percent obligated	70	17	10	1	2	0
Percent spent (outlays)	15	31	27	13	7	0

Sources: Obligation rates from Department of Defense, *Financial Summary Tables, Fiscal Year 1987*, tab L; outlay rates from table 3.

structure—for example, by not buying unneeded weapons. It is also important, however, not to pay excessive prices for the weapons that are bought. Reforms—some of which have been proposed by the Department of Defense and congressional committees—are needed to eliminate excessive profits recorded by defense contractors.

These profits have risen dramatically during the Reagan administration, while the profits of comparable durable goods manufacturers have fallen; the former now exceed the latter by a considerable margin, as measured by the Defense Department itself (see table 20).[48]

In this era of the $7,000 coffee pot and $400 hammer, it is difficult to argue that higher efficiency explains the difference. Nor do higher profit margins appear to reflect higher risk on the part of the defense contractor; indeed, recent Pentagon-commissioned and Conference Board studies indicate that, in general, the contrary holds.[49]

While in the long term wholesale reform of the entire weapon-acquisition process may be in order, some immediate savings could be gained by three direct and limited reforms to raise efficiency.

First, Cost Accounting Standard (CAS) 414 could be revoked. In effect, CAS 414 allows defense contractors to bill the Defense Department for interest on loans taken for investment in facilities, a practice that requires arduous auditing and has not been shown to reduce prices or stimulate investment.

48. A recent Navy study of 22 weapon manufacturers "found that their profits were more than twice as high on military contracts as on sales to their commercial customers." Bill Keller, ". . . And Some Bargain Hunting at the Pentagon," *New York Times*, February 9, 1986.

49. Patrick J. Davey and Francis J. Walsh, Jr., "Financial Community Perceptions of the Defense Industry: 1985," prepared for the Logistics Management Institute (New York: Conference Board, March 1985); and Myron G. Myers and others, "Facilities Capital as a Factor in Contract Pricing," prepared for the Department of Defense (Bethesda, Md.: Logistics Management Institute, May 1985).

Table 20. **Profits: Defense versus Comparable Durable Goods, 1970–83**

Percent

	Profit measured as:			
	Return on assets		Return on sales	
Category	1970–79	1980–83	1970–79	1980–83
Department of Defense business	19.4	23.3	6.0	7.4
Durable goods	14.4	10.6	8.0	5.9

Source: Department of Defense, *Defense Financial and Investment Review* (GPO, 1985), pp. V-30, V-32. Figures do not include government-financed independent research and development, bid and proposal (IR&D/B&P), which doubled to $3 billion between 1980 and 1984. Were these government payments included as profits—as they are for commercial business—the DOD return-on-sales figures would be higher by about 3.5 percentage points.

Second, profits now permitted on general and administrative overhead expenses could be eliminated, as proposed by the Defense Department. The Senate Armed Services Committee has also shown considerable interest in such a reform.

Third, as part of the elimination of profits on general and administrative expenses, lower ceilings on the department's financing of independent research and development, bid and proposal (IR&D/B&P), could be instituted, as proposed by the House Appropriations Committee. This spending is supposed to underwrite internal research and development *not* associated with any specific defense project. It is hard to monitor. More important, direct Defense Department funding of research and development is already extraordinarily high.

Four-year savings from these modest procurement reforms are estimated in table 21; they total more than $13 billion in budget authority and more than $8 billion in outlays.

Recovery of the "Inflation Dividend"

Finally, beyond these policy recommendations, there is a further volume of savings that, in principle, is possible. Between fiscal 1982 and 1986, nearly $28 billion was appropriated to cover anticipated inflation that never materialized. Because inflation was lower than anticipated, appropriations were higher than necessary (see table 22).

Perhaps President Dwight D. Eisenhower overstated the case when he said, "every gun made, every warship launched, every rocket fired signifies a theft from those who are hungry, unfed, and unclothed." But

Table 21. Savings from Procurement Reforms, Fiscal Years 1987–90
Billions of dollars

Action	1987	1988	1989	1990	Total
Revoke Cost Accounting Standard 414[a]	1.7	1.7	1.8	1.9	7.1
Disallow profits on general and administrative overhead[b]	0.8	0.8	0.9	0.9	3.4
Freeze IR&D/B&P ceiling[c]	0.7	0.7	0.7	0.7	2.8
Savings in budget authority[d]	3.2	3.2	3.4	3.5	13.3
Savings in outlays[d]	0.8	1.9	2.6	3.0	8.3

a. Savings from revocation of CAS 414 are estimated as 1.2 percent of the sum of procurement (P) and research, development, test, and evaluation (R) budget authority in each year. P + R budget authority data from *Historical Tables, Budget of the United States Government, Fiscal Year 1987*, table 5.1. The 1.2 percent is based on 1983 *Defense Financial and Investment Review* results: allowable CAS 414 interest was 1.5 percent of the sales ($65,552.4 million) examined by *DFAIR*. Department of Defense, *Defense Financial and Investment Review*, app. vol. 1: *Touche Ross Study* (GPO, 1985), p. VI-29. These sales represented only *major* contractors and accounted for roughly 68 percent of Defense Department sales, if one estimates the total as the value of P + R spending obligations *actually entered into* in a given year, $96.6 billion in 1983. Computed using obligation rates from Department of Defense, *Financial Summary Tables, Department of Defense Budget for Fiscal Year 1985* (DOD, 1984), tab N. Assuming that the ratio of total sales to P + R budget authority ($103.2 billion in 1983) is constant at 94 percent (1983's value), the CAS 414 revocation saves between 1.5% of 68% of 94% of P + R (if small contractors are excluded) and 1.5% of 100% of 94% of P + R (if small contractors benefit proportionately). The 1.2 percent figure is the average of these factors.

b. General and administrative (G&A) savings begin with the same yearly estimate of total sales (94 percent of P + R). The average markup of G&A is 7 percent. Department of Defense, *Defense Financial and Investment Review*, p. V-17. Seven percent of 94 percent of P + R, net of any reduction in IR&D/B&P ($0.7 billion in fiscal 1987), is the G&A base. Profit on this base is what is disallowed; the Defense Department estimates the profit rate at 8 percent; the Navy at 9.2 percent. Again, the average is used, 8.6 percent. Tom Burgess, "Navy, DoD Studies Differ on Contractors' Profits," *Navy Times*, December 16, 1985.

c. The $0.7 billion IR&D/B&P figure is the fiscal 1986 Defense Department ceiling, adjusted for inflation, minus my proposed level of $5.0 billion. Defense Department ceiling from *Department of Defense Appropriation Bill, 1986*, H. Rept. 99-332, 99 Cong. 1 sess. (GPO, 1985), pp. 284–85.

d. Aggregate outlay rates for the investment accounts are used to translate these budget authority savings into outlay savings. These are derived as explained in the appendix, and equal 0.24, 0.34, 0.21, 0.10, and 0.05 on a five-year basis. Underlying budget authority data and outlay rates for the individual accounts are from Department of Defense, *Financial Summary Tables, Fiscal Year 1987*, tabs A, M.

when nearly $28 billion is appropriated and there are not even any weapons to show for it, change is essential, especially considering the alternative uses to which such monies might be put in our society. The recovery of whatever monies remain—look under unobligated balances and reprogramming—should be ordered.[50]

Conclusions

Secretary of Defense Weinberger is correct when he insists that defense spending is driven to a unique extent by external—and especially

50. Since, as a practical matter, their recovery is unlikely, no such savings are included in the adjustments proposed in table 23.

Table 22. Estimated Dividends in the Defense Budget Due to Inflation Overestimates, by Appropriation Title, Fiscal Years 1982–86

Billions of dollars

Appropriation title	1982	1983	1984	1985	1986	Total
Military personnel	0.10	0.22	0.18	0.12	0.01	0.63
Operation and maintenance	1.75	2.84	2.65	1.52	0.05	8.81
Procurement	3.83	4.92	3.79	2.23	0.12	14.89
Research, development, test, and evaluation	0.62	0.87	0.75	0.52	0.04	2.80
Military construction	0.26	0.18	0.14	0.10	0.01	0.69
Total	6.56	9.03	7.51	4.49	0.23	27.82

Source: General Accounting Office, *Potential for Excess Funds in DOD* (GAO, 1985), app. 6, p. 11.

Soviet—factors, and that the defense budget, in turn, should not be held hostage to the deficit. Rather, it must be based on a rigorous and sober assessment of the East-West balance of military power and on prudent choices in meeting military needs. Unfortunately, the Reagan defense program falls short of this standard and continues to manifest six disturbing traits:

— An exaggerated assessment of Soviet military power, one based largely on static and oversimplified measures of military strength;

— An underassessment of U.S. and allied efforts, which, combined, have outstripped those of the Soviets and their allies for the last two decades;

— The adoption of strategies that, if feasible at all, are inefficient in accomplishing basic military tasks and that elevate needlessly the risk of escalation (for example, the maritime strategy);

— Excessive growth rates in programs of dubious urgency (for example, the ''enhancement of deterrence'' through strategic defenses);

— Wasteful redundancies (such as in the bomber/cruise missile leg of the strategic triad); and

— Payment of uncompetitive prices.

Options

It seems unlikely that, at this late juncture, much discipline will be imposed on the Defense Department from within. Congress's options, in the very largest sense, are therefore three.

One option is to approve the president's budget as submitted, continuing to indulge a costly confusion between ''what you pay'' and ''what you get.''

A second option is to reject the president's budget, but to construct no alternative and—through deadlock—to risk triggering the irrational ravages of Gramm-Rudman-Hollings when, in August 1986, the Office of Management and Budget and the Congressional Budget Office estimate the federal deficit for fiscal 1987.

A third option is to chart a middle course, embark on a multiyear revision of the president's budget, and put defense on a more efficient, sustainable path. Based on dynamic assessments of the nuclear and conventional military balance, the adjustments set forth in table 23 represent one such alternative, which would reduce outlays over four years by $117.1 billion.

Recommendations

Though grouped into clusters, or modules, the recommendations given there could be adopted in isolation. Since, as a practical matter, recovery of the so-called inflation dividend is unlikely, no such saving is assumed. Neither have I included the substantial savings that might accrue through changes in fuel prices, or through the thousand-and-one tiny cuts in which Congress is so practiced. In short, the specific changes proposed in the table are not exhaustive. Rather, they represent major force structure (and pricing) alternatives of the sort that can be derived from considerations of strategy and from the analysis of major force planning contingencies. The changes also focus on the investment accounts (procurement, research and development, and military construction). Investment reductions in fiscal 1987 translate into large outlay savings in the future, permitting deficit reduction to unfold without plundering readiness, a problem that reflects the peculiar dynamics of "slow" versus "fast" defense outlays discussed at the outset.

In the strategic nuclear realm, the stealth *technologies* are funded (for example, through the advanced cruise missile program) while the procurement of redundant *platforms*, such as the Stealth (advanced technology) bomber, is not. Similarly, a stable program of research into strategic defenses is as prudent as a crash program is wasteful. On the offensive front, credible deterrence requires retaliatory options far more discriminating and flexible than the wholesale destruction of Soviet society, although the ultimate capacity to retaliate massively should never be in doubt. The changes proposed in table 23 would not call into question the credibility of America's strategic deterrent. A high degree of retaliatory dexterity is assured, including substantial "prompt" and "delayed" hard-target kill capabilities and broad countermilitary potential.

Tactical air forces and ground-based air defenses expand and modernize at an adequate pace while the "tacair" mix is shifted away from the F-15E and the deep-attack strategy (including emerging technologies) toward the less-expensive, multipurpose F-16, supplemented by upgraded F-4s and measures to enhance defensive effectiveness and airbase survivability.

Ground forces also modernize at an adequate pace; the drift toward light divisions is stopped in a way that does *not* jeopardize conventional deterrence in the Persian Gulf and, by creating a new division, enhances it in Central Europe. There, defensive advantages are further magnified through terrain modifications, instant antitank ditches, and other inexpensive measures. Adequate sustainability and readiness are provided, while global mobility is increased through sealift procurement.

Other naval growth rates are reduced to levels consistent with the twelve carrier battle-group force structure that is needed to execute the Navy's essential missions efficiently. In particular, the chimera of a Nelsonian *surface* naval victory at Murmansk—the maw of Soviet maritime power—is abandoned, and with it the prime justification of the fifteen-carrier fleet and all its surface, subsurface, and tactical air accoutrements. The maritime strategy's other basic component—forward conventional submarine operations against Soviet strategic ballistic missile submarines—is also sufficiently questionable as to warrant some budgetary restraint (evident in the deferral of procurement funding for the SSN-21 attack submarine). None of these changes jeopardize the Navy's ability to protect the sea lanes in wartime or to support U.S. foreign-policy objectives in peacetime.

Savings from the implementation of the proposals set forth in table 23 would total $171.2 billion in budget authority and $117.1 billion in outlays over four years. While these alterations in the Reagan administration's defense plan were not generated in an uncritical effort to reduce the deficit, they would contribute significantly to its reduction, without detriment to the security of the United States or its allies.

Table 23. Proposed Alterations to the Administration's Defense Plan, Fiscal Years 1987–90

Billions of dollars of budget authority unless otherwise specified

Program	Action	Savings				
		1987	1988	1989	1990	Total
Strategic nuclear						
Strategic Defense Initiative	Freeze at fiscal 1985 level[a]	3.3	4.7	5.6	6.9	20.5
Antisatellite (ASAT) program	Freeze development; cancel procurement funds	0.1	0.4	0.4	0.5	1.4
MX missile	Cap at 50; reduce test procurement to 12 a year	1.0	1.6	1.1	1.1	4.8
Small ICBM (Midgetman)	Freeze at fiscal 1985 level[b]	0.9	2.1	2.7	3.3	9.0
Stealth (advanced technology) bomber (ATB)	Cancel procurement funds; hold in reduced development	2.1	4.0	4.0	5.0	15.1
Other stealth capabilities	Reduce growth rate by 50 percent/defer advanced tactical fighter (ATF) until 1989	1.3	1.3	1.3	1.4	5.3
Army/Air Force						
F-15E/F-16/F-4 tactical aircraft	Terminate F-15E/alter F-16 model mix/upgrade F-4[c]	2.9	2.2	2.4	2.1	9.6
Selected emerging-technology (ET) programs[d]	Cancel or cancel procurement funding	1.7	2.0	2.0	2.0	7.7
Airbase survivability	Expand current program	-0.1	-0.1	-0.1	-0.1	-0.4
Patriot air defense missile	Reduce growth rate to 400 a year	0.4	0.4	0.6	0.3	1.7
Army helicopter improvement program (AHIP)	Cancel[e]	0.3	0.2	0.4	0.4	1.3
M1 Abrams tank	Reduce growth rate to 540 a year[f]	0.8	0.8	0.6	0.0	2.2
M2 Bradley fighting vehicle	Cancel; replace with improved TOW vehicle (ITV) and upgraded M113[e]	0.8	0.6	0.3	0.3	2.0
Fort Drum	Terminate light division military construction	0.2	0.3	0.4	0.0	0.9
Low-tech defensive preparations	Instant antitank ditching; terrain modification; prechambering	-0.2	-0.2	0.0	0.0	-0.4
Airlift/sealift						
C-17 aircraft	Cancel	0.2	1.4	2.3	3.6	7.5
TAKRX fast sealift ship	Expand at 2 a year	-0.2	-0.2	-0.2	-0.2	-0.8
Navy						
SSN-21 nuclear attack submarine	Cancel procurement funds	0.5	0.2	1.7	0.5	2.9

SSN-688 nuclear attack submarine	Reduce growth rate to 2 a year	1.2	0.7	0.7	1.5	4.1
DDG-51 (Arleigh Burke) destroyer	Reduce growth rate by 2 a year	1.7	1.6	1.7	1.8	6.8
CG-47 (Aegis) cruiser	Reduce growth rate by 1 a year	1.0	1.0	1.0	1.0	4.0
Nuclear aircraft carrier (CVN)	Forgo service life extension program (SLEP); put 3 in reserve	1.6	2.1	1.7	1.9	7.3
Auxiliary ships	Cut for 12 aircraft carrier battle groups (CVBGs)	0.7	0.2	0.8	0.2	1.9
F-14, F/A-18, A-6 aircraft; SH-60 helicopter	Cut for 12 aircraft carrier battle groups (CVBGs)	2.8	3.0	2.6	2.5	10.9
V-22 aircraft	Cancel[e]	0.4	0.6	0.8	1.2	3.0
Sustainability, readiness, procurement						
Modern munitions (excluding AMRAAM)	Impose real freeze	1.5	1.6	2.2	1.7	7.0
AMRAAM (advanced medium-range air-to-air missile)	Cancel[e]	0.8	1.1	1.2	1.1	4.2
Operation and maintenance (O&M) housekeeping functions	Impose real freeze	2.9	3.8	5.1	6.6	18.4
Procurement reform	Eliminate uncompetitive profits	3.2	3.2	3.4	3.5	13.3
Total savings in budget authority	...	**33.8**	**40.6**	**46.7**	**50.1**	**171.2**
Resulting levels of budget authority	...	277.8	291.8	306.8	324.6	1,201.0
Percent real budget authority growth (year-to-year)[g]		−2.9[h]	+1.6	+0.5	+1.1	+0.1[i]
Total savings in outlays	...	**14.4**	**25.9**	**34.8**	**42.0**	**117.1**
From reductions in fiscal 1987–90 budget authority[j]		10.4	23.6	33.8	41.6	109.4
From rescissions of prior-year budget authority[k]		4.0	2.3	1.0	0.4	7.7
Resulting outlay levels	...	274.1	281.9	291.0	303.1	1,150.1
Percent real outlay growth (year-to-year)[l]		+3.3	−0.2	−1.2	−0.5	+0.4[i]

Sources: Calculated using data from *Department of Defense Annual Report, Fiscal Year 1987*; Department of Defense (DOD), *Financial Summary Tables, Fiscal Year 1987*; DOD, *Program Acquisition Costs by Weapon System, Department of Defense Budget for Fiscal Year 1987* (DOD, 1986); DOD, *Procurement Programs (P-1), Department of Defense Budget for Fiscal Year 1987* (DOD, 1986); DOD, *R,D,T&E Programs (R-1), Department of Defense Budget for Fiscal Year 1987* (DOD, 1986); Office of the Secretary of Defense, *Operation and Maintenance Overview, Fiscal Year 1986* (DOD, 1985); Office of the Assistant Secretary of Defense (Comptroller), *National Defense Budget Estimates for FY 1986; Historical Tables, Budget of the United States Government, Fiscal Year 1987*; CBO, *Budgeting for*

Table 23—*continued*

Defense Inflation (CBO, 1986); CBO, "The MX Missile Test Program and Alternatives," Staff Working Paper, February 1986; CBO, *Costs of Expanding and Modernizing the Navy's Carrier-Based Air Forces* (CBO, 1982); CBO, *Tactical Combat Forces of the United States Air Force: Issues and Alternatives* (CBO, 1985); and congressional sources. Figures are rounded.

a. $1.4 billion. *Department of Defense Annual Report, Fiscal Year 1987*, p. 223.

b. $0.5 billion. Ibid., p. 215.

c. Equivalent to option IIIB of CBO, *Tactical Combat Forces*, pp. 36, 37, 41–45.

d. Cancels procurement funding for JSTARS (Joint Surveillance and Target Attack Radar System) and LANTIRN (Low-Altitude Navigation and Targeting Infrared System for Night); cancels Aquila, PLSS (Precision Location Strike System), JTIDS (Joint Tactical Information Distribution System), and the terminally guided weapon variant of the MLRS (Multiple-Launch Rocket System); and reduces by 50 percent the growth rate of JTACMS (Joint Tactical Missile System).

e. For excellent discussions, see CBO, *Reducing the Deficit: Spending and Revenue Options* (GPO, 1986), pp. 38, 41–42, 46–47, 50–51.

f. This growth rate provides for efficient two-shift peacetime production at the Lima, Ohio, plant, with the Detroit facility available for wartime surge. It also ensures complete modernization of the active forces, plus a war reserve of 60 days, assuming a wartime tank attrition (irreparable) rate of 1 percent a day (not including any of the more than 4,000 M60 tanks in the U.S. inventory).

g. Computed using composite inflation rates given in CBO, *The Economic and Budget Outlook: Fiscal Years 1987–1991* (CBO, 1986), p. 110.

h. Computed using fiscal 1986 enacted as base. If, as recommended, $9.3 billion were rescinded from 1986 budget authority, and the resulting budget authority of $269.1 billion were taken as the base, real growth in 1987 would be +0.4 percent.

i. Average.

j. For outlay reductions from freezing O&M housekeeping, see table 17, and from procurement reform, see table 21. Outlay reductions from the proposed action on nuclear aircraft carriers were computed from the given budget authority reductions using composite O&M outlay rates from DOD, *Financial Summary Tables, Fiscal Year 1987*, tab M. The remaining outlay reductions were computed from the given budget authority reductions using aggregate outlay rates for the investment accounts, derived as specified in ibid., tabs A, M. Those aggregate outlay rates are, by year, 0.24, 0.34, 0.21, 0.10, and 0.05.

k. For details, see table 18.

l. Computed as in note g. As its base, the calculation takes the fiscal 1986 outlays given in *Budget of the United States Government, Fiscal Year 1987*, p. 5-5, but uses outlays as computed by the author in table 2 for fiscal 1987–90.

Multiyear Programming of Budget Authority and Outlays

CONCERN WITH deficit reduction has focused attention on the problem of estimating the changes in budget authority that are necessary to achieve *specified* changes in outlays in a given year. There is a general, multiyear solution to this important problem.

Let us define a "first-year aggregate outlay rate," r_1, as the following ratio: the *sum* of the first-year outlays for each appropriation title, divided by the total budget authority for some base year; let us use fiscal 1987. The "second-year aggregate outlay rate," r_2, let us define as the sum of the second-year outlays for each appropriation title, divided by the total budget authority *for the same base year,* 1987. One would proceed in the same way to compute third-, fourth-, and fifth-year outlay rates, r_3, r_4, and r_5. These coefficients allow one to estimate the pace at which total fiscal 1987 budget authority is paid out over five years. Implicitly, the estimate assumes there is no change in the "market basket," or mix, among appropriation titles, an assumption that can be relaxed (see below).

In addition to outlays generated from current budget authority, a certain amount of spending would occur if budget authority were literally zero for each of the fiscal years 1987–91. This is the backlog of outlays resulting from budget authority granted in years prior to fiscal 1987. Denoting by PY_{87}, PY_{88}, and so on the spending in fiscal 1987–91 that results from budget authority (BA) granted prior to fiscal 1987 (see text table 4), the total outlays (OL) in each fiscal year from 1987 through 1991 are given by the master equations below.

Master Budget Authority/Outlay Equations

$$PY_{87} + r_1 BA_{87} = OL_{87}$$
$$PY_{88} + r_2 BA_{87} + r_1 BA_{88} = OL_{88}$$
$$PY_{89} + r_3 BA_{87} + r_2 BA_{88} + r_1 BA_{89} = OL_{89}$$
$$PY_{90} + r_4 BA_{87} + r_3 BA_{88} + r_2 BA_{89} + r_1 BA_{90} = OL_{90}$$
$$PY_{91} + r_5 BA_{87} + r_4 BA_{88} + r_3 BA_{89} + r_2 BA_{90} + r_1 BA_{91} = OL_{91}$$

Since the PYs and r values are constants calculated in advance, and since the outlays on the right are targets specified by the analyst, the derived budget authority requirements (denoted below with asterisks) can be obtained by simple repeated substitution. From the first equation,

$$BA_{87}^* = \frac{(OL_{87} - PY_{87})}{r_1}.$$

Substituting this into the next equation, we obtain

$$BA_{88}^* = \frac{(OL_{88} - PY_{88} - r_2 BA_{87}^*)}{r_1}$$

and so on, for BA_{89}^* through BA_{91}^*.

Thus for any specified outlay trajectory, the requisite budget authority trajectory can be derived.

Of course, the same master system of equations can be run "forward," beginning with a budget authority schedule, to estimate the outlay stream that results.

The system can be disaggregated to whatever extent is desired. For example, it applies *exactly* to each appropriation title (such as the procurement account, if all numbers, outlay rates included, are for that account alone). No assumption about a fixed market basket is implicit in that case.

Intermediate aggregations are also possible. Rather than the budget authority–wide outlay rates developed at the outset, or the account-specific rates (such as procurement) one would use if one were applying the master equations to a single account, one can develop other outlay rates.

For example, first-year aggregate outlay rates for the investment accounts (procurement, R&D, and military construction) as a group can be developed, and analogous outlay rates for the operation and support (O&S) accounts (operation and maintenance, military personnel, and family housing) as a group can be developed. The first-year outlay rate for investment would be the sum of the first-year outlays for the investment accounts (procurement, R&D, and military construction) divided by total investment budget authority in fiscal 1987; the second-year investment outlay rate would be the sum of the second-year outlays for the investment accounts divided, again, by the base-year (fiscal 1987) investment budget authority, and so on. Strictly analogous computations would yield aggregate O&S outlay rates.

Using these, the master equations can be applied, separately, to investment and O&S groups, permitting rather refined programming. For instance, one could specify that investment and O&S *outlays* are to grow in such a way that, year-to-year, O&S acquires a larger percentage of total outlays (that is, proportions change over time). The investment and O&S *budget authority* schedules required to satisfy this outlay plan can then be obtained directly from the master equations for each group (investment and O&S), with budget authority cuts and additions orchestrated accordingly.

A given five-year defense plan can be parsed in any number of ways using this general procedure: by service, by contingency, or into familiar categories such as readiness, modernization, force expansion, and sustainability, or into entirely new categories. Rather high-resolution outlay planning can be translated into a budget authority plan by this means.